· · ·

The Little Book of Divorce Wisdom

Perspectives After Rebuilding:
People Open Up About Splitting Up

By Holly M. Russo

· · ·

Publisher: Wavian Arts Publishing
Savage, MD
wavianarts@gmail.com

Copy editors: Rebecca Coleman and David Aretha
Interior design: Eric Goss and Linda Mahns
Cover Design: Holly M. Russo
Sanity keeper, confidante, best friend, partner and amazing human: Rich Morey
Illustration: Anne-Claire Regan, Hibou Designs
Cartoons: CartoonStock.com
Poems: Albert Huffstickler, Marty McConnell, and John Roedel
Quotes: Janine Kwoh, L.R. Borbón, Dr. Nicole LePera, and Esther Perel

Acknowledgments: *To all who shared their stories to help others, thank you. Your insight helps make a lonely and overwhelming experience less so:* Amy, Angela, CP, DeeDee, EB, Gerri, Gillian, Jesse, Jason, Jenna, Kimberly, Maria, Mel, Melissa Ann, Michele, MLA, Nicole, Rich, and Tim, and the rest who wished to remain anonymous.

ISBN: 979-8-9877362-0-3
Library of Congress Control Number: 2023901890
Ed: 1

Disclaimer

This book is not intended as a substitute for professional advice. It is not meant to replace, countermand, conflict, or substitute for the advice given to you by your own medical, financial, legal, or mental health service providers. The author and publisher disclaim all liability in connection with the use of this book.

NOTE: *If you need help, please seek the advice of a professional. If you're in the U.S. and not sure who to call, dial "211" in any state and they will direct you to appropriate resources.*

For Mom

I'm sorry you didn't get a chance to see me finish this, but you always believed in me anyway. I promise to carry your torch and do whatever I can to make the world a kinder place.

To Rich

Thank you for being my happily-ever-after.

Table of Contents

Hurricane Sandy aftermath, Union Beach, New Jersey (2012)

Introduction

When Hurricane Sandy ripped through New Jersey and tore houses in half, I began thinking about how obvious the rebuilding process is when you can see it so clearly. There's home: a pile of broken lumber. Nowhere to sleep. It takes time to recover from that. And even then, some things may be lost forever.

No one expects rebuilding a home to be instantaneous but I think people hope to rebound fairly quickly from a breakup. Yet it's not that different, really.

When a union crumbles, each half must rebuild. Where you once lived—together, in the fused universes of your lives—has been razed to the ground. You must begin at an end.

I wrote this book because I had to start over. I didn't fully understand what went wrong or where to begin. I didn't know how to pick up the pieces. I didn't know ME.

Breakups are so commonplace that they can seem almost trivial, but our lives are structures that we build, like homes. Starting over can be all-consuming. And there's no City Hall to ensure sound building code, watch for fire hazards, or make sure we include the right load-bearing walls. We must learn to rebuild with no manual. But information is out there. Not just opinions, but research! The more I learned, the more I longed to help others.

I began special educator training by attending workshops held by the Gottman Institute, a research organization that focuses specifically on couples. Educators are not counselors but we can inform and guide people much like driving instructors, school tutors, financial advisors, business coaches, exam test trainers, and career mentors.

Through educator training, I learned:

- Most couples wait six years after trouble starts before even seeking counseling.
- Less than 10% of people who divorce sought counseling when they were in trouble.
- It's much easier to *prevent* unhappiness in a marriage than fix it when it arises.
- It's not enough to learn communication or conflict-resolution skills; the connection needs to be re-established too.
- Disconnection is the number one cause of dissatisfaction in a marriage.
- Why do couples fight? It's mostly over missed attempts at connection.
- People feel content when their lives have meaning, not just happiness. We are a meaning-seeking species, not a happiness-seeking one.

When I realized that only a fraction of those who needed help sought it, and that they waited that long, it was very eye-opening. That was me.

I vowed to write the book I needed to read.

All our lives, we are constantly faced with building and rebuilding. We build relationships with friends, colleagues, family, neighbors, and partners. We build careers, skills, jobs, habits, and routines. Sometimes they fall apart and we need to start over, and sometimes we just need to patch up some drywall.

The things we build, we must tend to. Nothing is ever built once and then is okay to leave alone. We must maintain our homes or they'll fall apart. Same with our bodies. And our relationships. We are never done assembling structures, repairing them, and rearranging them. We spend all our lives building and rebuilding. That's part of being alive.

The wise contributors to this book answered a survey about what they wish they had known before separating from their partners. The survey was not scientific; it was just people voluntarily sharing their personal experiences. While we often gain insight from other people's journeys, no two people will have exactly the same experience. No one will have the same feelings, issues, challenges, or outcomes. Each breakup is different. Keep this in mind as you read through this book.

I hope the insights shared here can help you tap into the power of your own resilience. Almost everyone who shared their wisdom appreciated what they learned about themselves and felt hopeful about the future. I hope you can feel that too.

> *remember you*
> *are not you, now. you are you*
> *a year from now. how does that*
> *woman walk? she is not sick or sad.*
> *doesn't even remember today.*
> *has been to Europe. what song*
> *is she humming? now. right now.*
> *that's it.*
> ~Marty McConnell, Survival Poem #17

You are not alone.

ABUSE WARNING:

If your relationship is abusive, do NOT go to couples counseling. Abuse is not a relationship problem. Counseling helps couples understand each other and gain perspective. It cannot fix the uneven power structure characteristic of an abusive relationship. Learn more at https://www.thehotline.org/identify-abuse/power-and-control or call the National Domestic Violence Hotline at 1-800-799-SAFE (7233) or dial 211.

. . .
Part 1

Painful Lessons

. . .

"Before we get going, is this the Big One?"

Chapter 1

What do you wish you had known, understood, or realized about divorce or separation ahead of time that would have made it easier to go through?

"That divorce is appropriate, beneficial, and even wise in certain situations."

"I wish I had known that a lot of my fears about it wouldn't come true—I was so afraid of being judged, losing friends, sinking into poverty, and being alone ever after, but my fears of how badly things might turn out were unfounded."

"The thing I want women in abusive relationships to know is how to recognize when they are in one, and that it is an **unfixable** situation, and not to burn through years of their lives struggling to make it work. It is TRAGIC that I stayed with my husband 15 years. Those were my best years—best work years, best reproductive years, best fitness years—and I spent them in a haze of self-destructive pain and depression and anger because I thought it was righteous to endure endless crap and keep leaning in to a marriage that was literally killing me. So, just because a guy has a disorder, or some emotional issue or other deserving compassion, he is not entitled to consuming the best years of your precious life that are over before you know it. Amend, amend, amend!"

"That my partner would eventually be okay. I thought I ruined his life (and did for a while), but eventually he healed and now appears to be the happiest he's ever been."

"We live in a 'No Regrets!' culture so women try not to feel regret, let alone admit it to their friends, or the world. If it helps one other woman, I'll do it: At 58 (Jesus I'm old!)—fifty frickin eight—I found love again, so yay, it can happen blah blah blah, but while it beats being lonely, finding it at last doesn't make it all OK. I deeply regret that I did not find him, or another kind, decent, loving, devoted man, to have a family with because I was busy being loyal and compassionate to a bunch of assholes. I hugely regret that I can not make babies with my wonderful guy and raise them together. We are too old now. I'm never going to have that rewarding family around me in my dotage that we built together. I will never have a golden wedding anniversary. Ladies, don't waste your time. You have way less of it than you think."

"I'm really liking how attachment theory predicts and explains why you can or can't seem to find a lasting relationship, and also who's a good bet and who ain't."

"Maybe just that although it was a difficult process, I would come out on the other end with a better life than I had before. It gets better!"

"I wish I could have recognized and understood Autism Spectrum Disorder (ASD). While recognizing ASD would have helped make things smoother, and possibly even prolonged or preserved the marriage, ultimately the marriage was unhealthy and unsafe for me and it still had to end—or never have been started—because I was also dealing with an entitled, abusive man. There is no cognitive therapy for that. It's not a neurology deserving of compassion. Sometimes there is more than one thing wrong."

You may not need a lawyer.

IF separation is mutual, and amicable, and trust and friendship are strong, and there are no children or complicated shared assets, you may be able to file for a petition for dissolution of marriage with your county clerk of court. However, it's still wise to consult with a lawyer to learn about what it means for your situation.

"I wish I would have known that I could have skipped hiring an attorney and just filed on my own."

"A good mediator will get you an identical deal to a courtroom for a fraction of the time and money."

"I wish I had known where to find reviews/advice for picking a mediator."

"[I wish I'd known] the expense. Mediators are expensive, but attorneys are even more expensive. And if there is a custody battle, the retainer increases. Time is money in the legal realm, and it ain't cheap."

"I wish I would have known that it isn't really required that you go through the child support office in order to get support. You can work it out between the two of you and keep that dang office out of the picture."

"Mediation is a viable path forward if you have a reasonable relationship with your former spouse. We actually used an online service to draw up the paperwork! It cost a total of $700, which we split."

"I wish I'd known that involving lawyers is the road to financial ruin and emotional hell. Using mediators or collaborative divorce or separation is far better. Also wish I'd known you can do your own divorce/separation because the law will support whatever the two of you agree on. So much better. I knew and benefited from being kind and respectful to my partners, whether or not we were in agreement and whether or not things were going my way, and that eased every aspect of dissolution. I am recently legally separated and took full advantage of this information as compared to my divorce years ago. As a result, my separation has been amicable, quick, satisfactory to both, and we have treated each other kindly and respectfully while not buying a Mercedes for any attorneys."

"Neither party wins by going to court, and [some] lawyers [may] do everything they can to convince you that you must litigate, especially by encouraging inflammatory feelings toward spouses—throwing gasoline on a fire."

"The system is set up to be adversarial. Each lawyer is trying to get the best outcome for their client and sometimes compromise is lost in that mix. What their lawyer is saying can sound like what your ex is saying, and you can lose your sense of actually talking to them. You may wonder, 'why are they asking for this?' but maybe something just got lost in translation."

It hurts.

"I never realized it could be so painful. There was no way to prepare for that and no way to turn back once I made a critical decision. When you are young, time seems endless, but reality only becomes relevant when the hourglass is low."

"Divorce is a death. It is hard, and it is OK to mourn. But there is life afterwards."

"I had spent at least a year making up lists of pros and cons, so I was well aware of the issues that would arise (money, losing friends, anger from child). I was told that 'it gets better'—and it does—but it was still awful when I was in the midst of it."

"I wish I had known how painful it would be when it was a done deal even though it was for the best."

"Nothing can prepare you for being blindsided."

"[I wish I had realized] that my former partner was hurting as much as me, or possibly more than me, when it came to ending our marriage."

It can take a while.

"It takes longer to heal than you think, even if you are the one who decided to walk away."

"Transitions take years."

The financial hardship is real.

"Get financial stuff in writing, always."

"I have never fully recovered."

"I wish I had known to have a prenup written before marrying and then have a postnup drawn up afterwards."

"For women [or anyone financially dependent], make sure they have their own savings set aside."

"Litigating [can] financially ruin a middle- or working-class family for the rest of their lives . . . [plus] the kids will have no college funds. BOTH partners must understand this,

BOTH partners must resolve not to be conned by family law attorneys; as soon as one partner gets taken in, the other gets dragged down as well."

"I wish I knew what [my] financial responsibility would be and laws associated with [that]."

The process can be overwhelming.

"As both the child and ex-wife of divorce, I wish I had understood the toll the legalities would take. The length of time, the stress and anxiety of the unknowns, the emotional impact."

"The incredible legal complexity varies from state to state. You think you can just get a divorce, then depending on your state you may not only need a cause but prove it, which makes things extremely difficult and contentious from the outset."

"The second time I divorced I had to stay in the marriage and convince him to move to a different state with more favorable divorce laws (that part was secret, of course) just to get out. Custody is also incredibly complicated. I wish I had known ahead of time to start keeping documents and journaling records of abuses so I'd have the evidence ready going into it."

"What is right and fair is not always the law."

"[I wish I had known] whether I truly needed a lawyer or not, the cost, how long it could take and why, what I 'deserved' (half the value of our house that I just walked away from to get away from him), how it would affect my credit score and debt load, how to go on with life afterward (without his income), and that I would lose almost all of my friends."

Be decent. It's okay to advocate for yourself. But be fair and kind.

"Don't try to take things out of spite."

"Do not make decisions while you are freshly hurting."

"Try and think through things you want/need in the separation without emotion on a practical level (tough, but might have saved some anguish). Remember to focus on you and your needs more than them and theirs."

"Nurturers and peace makers don't want to make waves, but there are times to walk away and [times to] fight. Fight for what is important, let small things go. Get comfortable with being uncomfortable—maybe cliché, but true. This is a rough period and we are stronger than we think. Lean on others for help. Get help . . . don't be afraid to ask for help. True friends step up, [and] others that aren't go away. And that's OK. (Painful, but OK.)"

"I wish I had known how to negotiate finances better. We had a moderator meet with us to go over our assets and divide out our debts, but I don't think I was in a good place to advocate for my financial security. Later a friend asked me why I didn't pursue alimony, and it was only because I worked and had my own salary and we did not have kids. Looking back, it was in my best interest to have gotten a better deal than just the proceeds of the sale of our house."

The pain can bring out everyone's worst.

"Early in the process, a stranger warned me that divorce would bring out the absolute worst in both sides; that any assumption of an easy, good-faith process was hopelessly naive. I assured myself that this wouldn't be the case with my ex and me, and then . . . it totally was. We were awful."

"One thing I wish I'd known is that I needed to prepare

for feelings of hatred and betrayal that I'd never imagined; that's the bummer. The good news is the other things I wish I'd known, or at least better understood: that divorce happens for a reason, it eventually ends, and if you get lucky and play your cards right, you come out of it significantly wiser, happier, and better positioned for happiness in future relationships."

"[I wish I had] realized that the abusive behaviors within the marriage would continue throughout the divorce."

"I tried to make it amicable while my ex hired a private investigator trying to find dirt on me . . . while she was cheating on me . . . she also took everything valuable out of the house and bank, even non-marital property all the way, including my birth certificates and things that had been lent to me by family . . . I got some of it back, but I didn't have a complete enough list."

"I wish I had been more conscious of the fact that at the point in time one decides to separate or divorce, in your heart you already know your partner and your own situation well enough to have the answer as to what kind of future relationship you are likely to have with them. Understanding this would have helped me to let go of my utopian TV fantasy earlier. It would have informed some of my decisions and enabled me to respond without taking on the added stress of trying to control the future by worrying about what my partner was experiencing, or how she would react in that moment of time."

"In my case, I had an acrimonious partner and I was fooling myself about the likelihood that we would 'stay friends' for the sake of the kids. Time will not heal the situation . . . ultimately any civility is based on a tenuous truce at best, with the slightest perceived injustice opening up the original wound to pour salt on it."

"The angrier or more scared the parties are, the more willing they are to part with tens of thousands of dollars to protect their children and their interests. It's the most emotional purchase you will ever make."

It can be lonely.

"[I wish I had known] how lonely you feel."

"I don't think there is anything that can really prepare you for the 'collateral damage' of divorce. No matter how much you realize and accept it as the best course for your family, the reaction of your parents (both sides) and children may be tough. Be prepared that your 'friends' are not going to want to get in the middle, so you may find yourself struggling alone. Your in-laws, [and] especially young children, have known you as Aunt/Uncle for years . . . are you still going to be or want to be in their lives?"

"I was divorced in my twenties and did not understand how divorce would create some isolation from my old social circles. There were many other friendships that were damaged by my divorce."

"[I wish I had known] that I would lose his entire family also."

"The social repercussions were almost worse than the financial ones."

Parenting can be harder.

"[I wish I had known] how hard it is to parent and deal with the questions of your child/children while dealing with your own emotions and stress!!!"

"The thing that came as the biggest surprise to me was how much my parenting relationship with my ex fell apart after he left. We had always been a great parenting team, and I expected that to continue even after he left. I had not anticipated that he would be so childish, resentful (even though he was the one who left), and histrionic about me, which made it so we couldn't be a family at all anymore or even communicate about parenting to any meaningful degree. I feel like this is an unusual outcome. It seems like either the father was crap to begin with and remained crap after he left, or else a good father attempts to stay a good father after he leaves. I feel like I inadvertently lied to my kids by telling them, when he left, that we would still do things as a family and they would be surprised at how little changed, when that isn't how it worked out at all."

"Seeing the pain your children go through was the hardest part of separation and divorce. I don't think anything could've prepared me for it."

"I don't think I would have let him go so easily if I'd known he'd become such a crap parent once he left. My marriage was not happy, but I would have been willing to swallow my feelings and deal with it for a few years longer if it meant my kids would still have a real father for a while. I didn't fight him very much about him leaving, and in retrospect, knowing what I know now, I would have made it much harder for him to go. I don't know if that ultimately would have been better for my kids, but I would have tried harder to (not physically!) beat some sense into him."

"If you know divorce is inevitable, don't prolong it because of the kids—it hurts everyone more to watch and go through the pain and emotions, especially if there's arguments and nastiness happening."

"I was a stay-at-home mom prior to being a single parent and I regret not doing much more to make sure I had a viable career to turn to so I could have supported myself right away. A huge amount of my stress in all this is wondering how I will even survive financially without my ex's support, and

I'm really kicking myself for thinking I could depend on a life with him and therefore didn't need to have a way to make my own money. And it's not like I thought a man should be the provider and the little woman should stay home and knit or whatever. I just thought we were a team, and that by making it possible for him to make the most of his career, I was doing my part for our mutual financial good. And I was, but little did I know he was going to run off on me. So if I could go back ten years and warn myself, I'd say 'get a freakin' job.'"

"[I wish I had known] what helps kids the most."

"If you have children, I can't recommend enough that you see a counselor or therapist who can help you shepherd them through the separation period and beyond. That may add more expense. It's worth it. It's best to start working with one ahead of breaking the news to them, because the counselor will help you with the best way(s) to do that. See the counselor by yourself if your spouse won't join you. It's going to be difficult for them. But I believe being honest with them about what's going on and your struggles, in a neutral and age-appropriate way, can really help them through it. You have to remain neutral. No spouse-bashing to the kids. Take the high road. Always. As they grow up, they'll understand more over time what this time was like for you. Right now, they just need help navigating this themselves. Their whole world is being upended, no matter how much you try to minimize the change to their lives. They need to feel the love and presence of both parents right now."

"[I wish I had known] the effect it would have on my children. My ex could not be alone and immediately found someone who was not that kind to my kids, but he put his needs first."

"I want to go back to how things were before we knew each other."

CartoonStock.com

Chapter 2

Is there anything you wish you'd been able to do differently?

Waiting out troubles can just end up prolonging the inevitable.

"I wish I would have realized it was over earlier [and] saved myself some time."

"Yes—left WAY WAY WAY WAY sooner."

"Find the strength to leave the relationship when I first knew it felt wrong. Because of the naiveté of youth, I was afraid of the implications and had a fear of change. I thought it was a phase and convinced myself that I would get used to it. This intensified once we were expecting—I began to worry that leaving would cause psychological damage to my (unborn) child. I made some personal choices before I finally decided to change my situation, and I still regret these indiscretions. I was not looking for another love and I never had a long-term side relationship, and when I finally came to see these dalliances as emblematic of larger issues in the relationship with my wife that were never going to go away, I knew I needed to leave the relationship in order to rebuild myself into the person I always wanted to be, but who lost his way at a young age and was not equipped with the wisdom or tools to help himself get back on the healthy path forward."

"Start [the divorce process] earlier."

"I wish I had been able to leave my marriage earlier, before my ex-wife (and daughter) found out that I was having an affair."

"I wish it had been easier to divorce sooner."

"I want to tell people, when it falls apart—when you *realize* it, at least—is not when it actually started to erode. The erosion starts small. It starts when you slip into fight or flight mode around your partner because of the frustrated sigh they heaved when you put on music they hate or when you asked a dumb question while watching a movie. The key to lasting love isn't eliminating quirks as much as it is respecting each other. Not grudgingly, but the embracing kind. You can feel the difference. You cannot act your way out of contempt."

"Leave sooner."

"Prepared more in advance. I tell friends now who think separating is on the horizon to save a bit."

Get good legal advice and know about options.

"Hire a better lawyer at the start."

"I wish I'd sought more information about divorce law."

"Know the type of lawyer to hire. I had to hire a different lawyer who didn't drag on the divorce. I had no kids. My first attorney didn't pay attention to me."

"We had a mediator, and at that point it was amicable. Once my ex met his girlfriend, he went to an attorney and from then on it was very expensive."

"I wish I'd reacted to threats sooner, particularly those involving custody. I basically stuck my head in the sand, waited to hire a lawyer, and hoped for the best until I was served with papers and told that the kids and their mom would be moving out of state. At that point, I had to slam the accelerator, hire the world's most expensive lawyer, and do a 180 on divorce's uniquely expensive intensity. It's just so hard to adjust to those crushing new realities as they happen."

"Do differently? No. Be seen and heard differently by the court system? Yes."

"Look up the process on my own to do it myself."

"I would have kept records and evidence of my husband's unacceptable behavior, instead of trying to be compassionate toward him. Because I threw away the evidence, I was later unable to get a custody order that would keep my child safe. Judges do not want to hear complainants' accusations about each other—they want to get through their docket, and the fastest way to do this is to assume the parties are both equally at fault. If one partner really did do something note-worthily horrible, you better have admissible documentation."

"[I wish] that the reduced separation before divorce time had been in effect when I was separated."

Be fair financially but also advocate for yourself and the kids.

"We did everything ourselves and there were no attorneys

involved. It was pretty amicable. The only regret is not putting college tuition in the divorce papers."

"I wish I had pressed for the sale of the house and possession of both of my dogs. I let him have both so I could be gone and done with him quicker (just 30 days to process uncontested and with no kids in my state). I would be richer and happier if I had pushed for what was legally mine."

"I just wanted to be away from him and didn't hold the divorce decree to task with splitting expenses. I didn't ask him for anything to help with the kids' schooling and extra money they needed. In a sense—I let him off 'scot-free.'"

"I wish I could have lifted my head out of the depression enough to be more proactive with financial outcomes."

"I wish I had fought for myself harder in my first marriage. I gave away too much emotionally and financially."

"[I wish I'd] been more assertive regarding asset division."

"He got off easy financially for all I put into the house/life together."

Build a support network and get help (especially in abusive and toxic situations).

"I would've reached out to more people for help."

"I wish I sought out professional counseling earlier than I did."

"Neither of us were healthy emotionally and had never learned good conflict resolution skills. We did everything wrong that relationship research says you're not supposed to do. We started out deeply in love, but love is not enough. You have to also be emotionally healthy (or learn to be so in counseling)."

"I wish I had chosen to take my time, chosen more compatible women to date long term, dated more women longer term, and learned better ways to express/maintain my desires."

"I wish I had been able to go into counseling right away instead of letting friends shape my 'exit strategy.'"

"My life coach and counselor has helped me heal so many parts of myself, but cost kept me from doing it sooner . . . some wounds take a very long time to heal when there is abuse."

"I wish I'd sought counseling on my own to unravel everything I was feeling before taking any steps."

"I wish I had believed my intuition when it was trying to warn me that something was very wrong. It would have saved more than just my own heart."

"Stop the abuse cycle and walk away. It's not worth it."

"Wish I had not been so angry. Had I been able to hold it together more, I probably could have been able to put on a better front for my kids and deal with his legal assaults."

"There were probably many things that I could have done, but separation appeared to be the only logical option at the time."

"Don't compare to others' highlight reel."

"I wish I could have kept my cool. I wish I had been able to control my negative emotions."

"This is complex, in that I was on a medication for a long time that changed my ways of thinking, my emotions, and my behavior, all for the negative. The choice before me was take it or possibly die faster. Looking back . . . I'd have rather not taken it. Stayed being my true me and enjoyed the time I had left with the person that I loved."

"Co-parent better."

"I wish I'd been able to get my exes to stop abusing drugs and alcohol. Barring that, I wish I'd been able to know, ahead of time, that I was entering relationships with men with drug and alcohol addictions, and choose other men who did not have these issues. I was raised without any addictions in the parental home, I don't drink or do drugs, and I was very naive."

"We had several separations, but I didn't let my family know the degree of my unhappiness, so the actual divorce was harder for many to accept. I think I didn't share earlier because I hoped we could mend our differences."

"[I would] not have made an agreement while I was hurting. I am super empathetic and I needed to be 'meaner.'"

"Wouldn't have gotten married! Ha."

"When things got heated, I wish I would've taken my mom's advice: 'Hang up the goddamn phone.' You don't have to take in what someone else is putting out. It's your choice what to absorb."

"I wish we could have remained in touch and I had been able to maintain a nice relationship with my mother-in-law. I was very fond of her, but my husband made it clear to sever all relationships we shared. I still miss her 15 years later (!), but she is now 85 years old, and I am pretty sure she's incapacitated. I wrote her a note last year when I mailed a lot of old family photos to her (my ex emailed me back to say to send them to her address), and she never wrote back to me, which is out of character for her. Her mother had had advanced dementia, so it is entirely possible that she does now too. When I was married, I thought my ex and I would take care of her in her old age, and I am sorry that didn't work out. I would have liked to do that, or in the case of our divorce, remain friendly. It wasn't possible."

"[I wish I had] protected myself more carefully from her abuse."

"[I wish I had] maintained communication."

Sometimes there isn't really anything that could have been done differently.

"I can't really complain, as things went pretty smoothly in the end. I can talk about what went right, which was that we communicated well and handled things as amicably as we could and made an effort to stay friends and be supportive to each other, which saved a lot on lawyer fees and grief and stress. We went into it with the attitude of 'how can we help each other and do right by each other?' instead of 'what can we get from each other?' or 'how can we hurt each other?' So I think that made all the difference and made it as easy as it could be."

"No. It was all necessary for my personal growth."

"Love cannot blossom when you don't feel revered. It begins to fray, like the reverse knitting of a sweater. First the ends come undone but it's still possible to neatly tuck the threads under. But eventually the core loses its structure and it's no longer recognizable. Being together no longer feels like home."

" I NEVER MEANT TO HURT YOU. "

Chapter 3

What has been the hardest part?

"Realizing I stayed too long."

"Going from making the decision to leave to actually walking out the door."

Starting over is tough.

"Learning how to live on my own, which I still suck at, because my earning potential is low due to a mental handicap and I never budgeted or tracked money until I was in my forties. Getting an apartment on my own was so difficult!"

"Starting over. Building a different life. Trying to find the right person for me."

"Losing some of my dearest friends. Most of your couple friends will choose a side, especially in the case of infidelity. Most did, and it wasn't mine. I was stunned at the time. Devastated. I've since forgiven and moved on, but it took quite a while. It was very difficult not having my closest friends around for support, especially in those early days."

"I'm married again. But I have new baggage from my first marriage, and new fears that I didn't have before. It feels incredibly unfair that my ex still has that much control."

"Learning to trust someone again was very difficult."

"The feeling of failure after having been so committed to making the marriage work."

The process itself can be grueling.

"Remaining under the same roof while you're trying to sell your home. That's hard!"

"The hardest part, I think, was the degree to which I didn't know myself—why I'd sabotaged the marriage, what I wanted (or should want) out of a relationship, what it would be like to be alone and independent. I needed therapy and medication and a hundred thousand hours' worth of conversations with trusted friends; thankfully, I sought out all three."

"Realizing that marriage is just business. That there isn't actually anything romantic about it and that when all is said and done, it's all about property and money."

"Not fully understanding why until years later. Everyone (partner included) wanted to know 'why,' but how could I explain when I didn't fully understand myself? It's also painful to think about the myriad 'better' ways it could have ended, but I wasn't evolved enough then. I wish I had understood so much more so I could have saved my partner from the nuclear side effects of my struggles."

"Knowing that I missed lots of warning signs, not protesting against her abuse more, not listening to my friends . . . I let her hurt a lot of people I care about, and I feel guilty about that."

"For me, [the hardest part] was the loss of my marriage and realizing my first husband wasn't who I thought he was."

"Still loving her. Even 10 years later. Missing her. For a long time I was dreaming about losing her over and over and over again. Knowing that I'd really rather not be with anyone else. Knowing that no matter what I do or say, she will very likely never talk to me again."

"Accepting that having a failed marriage behind me was not a blemish on my record. Also: anger management."

"The anxiety, and dealing with a rupture in my relationship with my (now 21-year-old) daughter (who was 19 and had just finished her first year of college when I moved out). It was hard, too, losing some friendships, and also going back to the synagogue that my (ex-) wife and I both belonged to, and either having to see people who were on 'her side' or having to see her there."

"I am over 20 years past my divorce, so it no longer feels hard. At the time, the rejection I felt was very challenging."

"The most difficult part initially was that we had recently got married and I rearranged my work life and moved tons of resources. We bought a house within the first six months before deciding to divorce, and all the uncertainty [was tough]. It was hard to grasp that I didn't lead the relationship and that I chose the wrong person to marry."

The effects on kids and family are hard to witness.

"Watching my daughter's heart break!!"

"Seeing my children struggle."

"Being a single parent."

"The hardest part at the time was having to clean up his mess and pay for his mistakes, even though we were no longer building a life together. Of course this has included the impacts of divorce on our son."

"Worrying about my son's life while he was in the mother's custody."

"Looking back (since it's been a lot of years ago), parenting. We had agreed that our children were a priority, but no matter how hard you try, it's difficult for young children to accept. Be prepared for resentment toward any new person who comes into their world."

"The hardest part was the first six months or so after separating, when I was adjusting to so many changes at once all while taking care of my daughter, who was still a toddler, with no family in the area to help—so all at once I was looking for a job after several years of not working, figuring out childcare, then adjusting to the new job with a crazy commute, then moving into a new place with no furniture and adjusting to a new commute, figuring out how to date as a single mom, and so on. I got really overwhelmed after six months, and then ended up readjusting the custody with my ex so that we would share the childcare 50-50 instead of me doing it all, and that helped a lot. It was a bit of a hurdle to admit to myself that I was overwhelmed and needed the help, because there's the societal expectation that, as the woman, you're supposed to be primary one responsible for the childcare—but I was lucky to have an ex who has turned out to be a great co-parent, and who was thrilled to have more time with our daughter. It ended up being a win-win to share the parenting time more, and I'm glad I got over the stereotypes about it, because otherwise I would have gone crazy!"

"The lawyers. All they want is to stir up trouble when there was very little."

"The toughest part was putting my life back together and helping my son to not be scarred by the experiences of my divorce from his father, and now my legal separation from his stepdad. I've never again found the feelings of love I had for the father of my child, and I continue to mourn even though I've moved on and been remarried a long time. The best days are the ones where I can feel grateful that I got to know what that love felt like, and I had it in my life for several years."

"Not seeing my kids daily."

"By far, it's been seeing my kids' relationship with their father go down the toilet. One by one, he's alienating all of our kids, and of course he thinks it's everybody else's fault but his. I feel powerless to do anything about it. If I go to him and say something about his interactions with the kids—something they were unhappy about, or that I see as a looming problem—he just bites my head off, and then he goes to the kids and confronts them with something like, 'Your mother said you're unhappy about this. Is that true?' Then of course they say no, no, it isn't, everything is fine, and he thinks I'm being a drama queen again, and the kid comes to me and says, 'Please don't try to "help."' It's pretty awful."

"Losing my in-laws."

"Being patient."

"Losing the friendly relationship we might have enjoyed as co-parents after his attorney convinced him to drop mediation and litigate. Our friendship could have survived mediation, but not the injuries inflicted upon me by my ex and his attorney during litigation. We were separated but still doing things together as a family, to our young child's delight and reassurance, until he switched. That changed our relationship from 'family' to 'enemies.' Meals, outings, gatherings with friends all went out the window. Even now that the hard part is long over and we can sit together companionably at a recital, trust, and the ability to be friends again someday, was destroyed."

"Knowing that while I made the decision to end this relationship, my daughter's life was also to be forever impacted. In the long run she is, I truly believe, safer and better for it—but that doesn't make it any easier, even years later."

"Raising children on my own with little support. My own family of origin is not a happy or healthy one. I suffered from depression while raising the kids. My son was very difficult, acted out, got arrested. It was a struggle for him growing up, it was a struggle for me, and he apologizes for it now, but I know it was hard for him. My daughter had depression. And hid it. Both my kids are now good, kind adults, and it was a long road. I am so proud of them."

"Perhaps the worst thing was my ex not attending my child's annual health checkups for a serious condition because he would not be in the same room as me. It was my kid's health, and he still would not do it. And his stepchild beating up my children and him not intervening because he would not cross his wife. It was hard to see my children hurt like this. I stopped sending them back to his home when they were preteens and put them in counseling, and he refused to participate and never told me why. He started, then just stopped responding. That was the end of my son's relationship with him. He believed his dad would step up."

Communicating with an ex can be challenging.

"The lack of cooperative co-parenting with respect to raising our kids has been the hardest part for me. I once remarked to a friend that the lack of communication from my (former) wife when the kids were with her or in any co-parenting situation was like I had a spouse who died. My friend replied, 'It's actually worse than that. If [she] was dead, you would have sole custody.'"

"Not having communication. He's not a very nice person and communication was NEVER in his vocabulary, but there has to be communication, especially when you have children."

"I have absolutely no idea how I could have guided this in a different direction from the beginning, [but] I really feel like it's just beyond his emotional range to not handle this so childishly. At the same time, I think that's by choice—I think it's a choice to refuse to grow or become better at this, so I stay angry about it because it could be different if he wanted it to be."

Financial repercussions can be severe.

"The financial ruin. Lost house in foreclosure, lost car to repossession, was homeless for four months, fell way behind in bills. Climbing out of [my] poor credit rating [is] nearly impossible."

"All the new normals, the debt, the loss, absolutely everything changed and didn't expect that."

"Watching my kids be neglected both emotionally and financially. We were a particularly bad case with regard to that."

Abusive and/or toxic behavior in a marriage can continue afterwards.

"The nightmares still pop up under stress about my ex. There are still parts of me needing healing. I still react and have feelings like with my ex due to the extended period of abuse. I still have a hard time speaking my feelings to my current spouse because of past abuse. (Thankfully, my spouse has been amazing when I'm afraid to speak my feelings . . . so in time I think this will pass.)"

"Waiting 366 days to file against my abuser and then having to wait [even more] for my ex to be tracked down and served."

"The fear. When someone is furious with you for leaving and wants vengeance and your personal destruction, and children are in the middle of it, and the other partner is not a safe parent, but it's only your word and you have no control over the outcome, and they're demanding your bank accounts and Facebook passwords and treating you like a criminal and you have no control. You simply have to ride the process out. The fear. The fear. The fear. I cannot overestimate how terrifying it is to be put on trial for wanting to leave a relationship. The judge has absolute power. He/she may be just as much of an asshole as your ex. They may not believe you. And they get to decide. Your worth and believability as a human, your worth as a parent, is all put on trial in such a way to deliberately paint you terribly, and it's just bottom-out awful."

"The longer it went on, the more stalking and harassment I endured."

"Still thinking about the marriage 15 years later, and my life now is SO MUCH BETTER. My ex-husband still occupies my thoughts, especially when I think about who I was in my twenties and thirties."

"Well, the children are grown up, married, divorced, and remarried. I guess our job is done."

Chapter 4

Is there something that might have prevented the relationship from ending?

Some said no.

"No. The first was a simple mismatch. I was 18. He did nothing wrong but it never would have lasted. The second two were both abusive."

"I don't think so."

"No, it never should have been a marriage in the first place. We were just good friends."

"No. He was a drug addict. He was unable to remain in recovery."

"No, it was abusive."

"No. There were 'red flags' from the beginning and I didn't listen to my gut."

"Only if he got treatment for mental health."

"Not marrying her in the first place."

"No. Our life goals and values weren't aligned. We shouldn't have married in the first place. Now I help people make better decisions about their life partners."

"Nope. He was physically abusive once when he twisted my arm trying to not let me leave an argument that was going nowhere. He was also verbally abusive all the time. I mean, my nickname to him was 'Bitch.' He was incredibly demeaning to me, putting his family, friends, and our dogs before me. He would say, 'You're not my friend, you're my wife,' which meant that I was well below them in the rankings. He neglected me by not being mentally present or caring, even when he wasn't deployed with the Air Force. While deployed to Kuwait for five months, he begged his best friend from high school to leave her husband, even though she was about to give birth to her first child any day, and marry him because he realized that he doesn't love me and never did. So, hell no! I wouldn't stay with him, not even when he realized that I was serious about leaving. The man-child cried and begged, but my boots were walkin', honey!"

"Not in this situation."

"I doubt it. My ex-wife was pretty much a master of three of Gottman's four horsemen of the apocalypse (criticism, contempt, and defensiveness). Maybe if we had gone into couples therapy a decade before we did, that might have helped. Maybe."

"Not at the time. We did the best we could with what we knew."

"Only [if there was] so much change by both of us that we would have had to be different people."

"Without the betrayal that ended our marriage, we'd most likely still be married—and sunken ever further into resentment, debt, terrible communication, and eventual full-on lovelessness. So the marriage could have been 'saved' fairly easily, only to preclude future happiness. What needed to happen was GROWTH, maturity, better communication, and an understanding that some relationships need to end for sad, entirely non-scandalous reasons."

"In my case, my ex later identified as a homosexual. So, the writing was on the wall."

"Nope, he was an abusive, narcissistic, selfish a**hole."

"Only if my ex had stopped drinking and drugging. Those things were out of my control, though, so we really did have to divorce. He was a danger to himself and our child."

"I don't think so. It was doomed from the start, but it took 14 years (!) to fully realize it. Pretty sad, really. When we married, four years into the relationship, I loved him but I wasn't in love with him. I think that had everything to do with it."

"I don't know. I can't imagine what it would have been. At the time, I saw no solution. Nothing at all."

"Looking back, I don't think so. Ultimately, the only thing that could have made a difference is never having been in the relationship in the first place. Although I have my own faults (belittling him, lack of respect for him), those arose from his poor behavior and poor choices (lying, cheating). The relationship ended when I discovered he was having an affair. He freed me from years of prior unhappiness by cheating. Then I could finally walk away."

Some said yes.

"Probably. You can always do more. I was so bitter and hurt that my wife left that I didn't give her any reason to come back."

"Learning better conflict resolution skills and emotional regulation skills. We both triggered each other all the time."

"Not the first marriage, but my second marriage, yes. We did not try therapy. I had a lot of baggage and I didn't feel right burdening him with it any longer."

"Yes, [it would have taken] two committed people!!"

"Yes. This is going to sound snotty or petulant, but I believe it's true: if I had stayed more subservient and not challenged him about things that were unacceptable or disrespectful, I believe we'd still be married. The problems really started when I developed a career, and he felt deeply threatened by the fact that I was making money and getting praise from others. If I'd never started that career, it would never have come up that he ordered me never to talk to him about my work again, which was the argument that I feel really revealed to me that this relationship could not last, because that's such an unreasonable thing to ask of your partner. And toward the end, if I hadn't pushed for us to have a functioning sex life, challenged his obsession with social media, things like that, he wouldn't have gotten fed up and left, I don't think. Does that mean I regret doing those things? No. I just recognize that divorce was the cost of doing those things, because of who I was married to."

"[If] my ex took marriage counseling seriously."

"Better communication."

"The relationship could have endured if I had submitted completely to the spouse's needs, but that would have meant enduring and condoning and keeping secret a lot of abuse, infidelity, and parasitism. In other words, there was no way to keep a healthy relationship from ending, but there was a way to keep a toxic relationship going, at great expense to me."

"Very early counseling and access to good therapy in the first couple years."

"There are many things that perhaps could have saved it. But I have come to believe no saving would have lasted."

"If I spoke up more instead of staying quiet so as not to cause drama, we could have had more useful conversations and possible solutions to issues of concern."

"Yes. We were in counseling with someone good, but she was very in your face. My husband did not like it and was dishonest in the meetings. She also revealed personal information of mine in group therapy in front of others, and I walked out and did not return. But I think she could have saved our marriage. My husband later told me he thought she could have."

"Possibly an understanding of Autism Spectrum Disorder (ASD) on both of our parts. Long, long after the divorce, we found we both are on the spectrum, which was likely at the core of many of our fights. And I was very angry at him for things he'd done. Maybe if I could have forgiven. But it was a lot and I was so angry."

"Very likely not being on a ridiculously high amount of a steroid that utterly changed my personality, made me gain weight, and had other negative effects for more than a year. And: being more patient. Being more supportive. Being more thoughtful. Being more kind."

"An increase instead of decrease of emotional expression of any sort from my husband as things got more difficult in my life [may have saved us]."

"Putting more effort into the relationship. We were too independent, and while this seemed great when we were first married because we were young and both used to single life, ultimately this proved to be part of our undoing, because as time went on, we were not creating and sharing enough joint experiences to keep us interested, connected, and growing together."

"Well, it had turned into a completely sexless relationship, with me having lost all attraction to my husband, so there were a few ways we could have gone. We talked about whether we should try having an open relationship and dating other people while still staying married and living together. But we both felt weird about that. Or we could have just resigned ourselves to continue having a sexless marriage. Or I guess I could have just viewed having sex as a duty or a job and done it even though I didn't want to, and I think my then-husband would have been fine with that option. I thought it might have helped me be physically attracted if my husband had been more romantically affectionate in ways that were not sex (kissing and holding hands, cuddling, etc.), and I tried to talk with him about it, but it just wasn't him at the time—he felt that if he was affectionate in those ways and it didn't lead to sex, it was like he'd been duped or wasted his time. So we just had a disconnect on the physical affection stuff, and I think the alternatives to splitting up would have been worse. I feel we made the best choice by ending it and giving each other the chance to start over."

"I'm granting your divorce and ordering you both be released back into the wild."

HARDIN

Chapter 5

Why did the relationship end?

Bad behaviors, communication patterns, mistreatment, and poor conflict resolution can build up over time.

"We fought too much. Too many power struggles to be 'right.'"

"He had a hard time accepting me. He looked down on my music, my education, my hobbies—just everything about me felt like it frustrated him. I began to feel smaller and smaller in his presence."

"My ex-wife was pretty much a master of three of Gottman's 'Four Horsemen of the Apocalypse'* (criticism, contempt, and defensiveness), which made communication—especially in fights—extremely difficult. From my perspective, our marriage started to go downhill when our daughter was born (when I felt criticized for not making more of an effort to give our daughter a bottle during the night); it was then 19 years before I moved out. On my side, I engaged in a lot of lying and concealing, which I think reflected a lack of confidence in myself and trust in my ex-wife."

"The relationship ended because my ex felt like I was too demanding and blamed him for everything, and as a result of those feelings, he turned to collecting women on social media who gave him attention and made him feel big and impressive. He asked for marriage counseling, but it turned out that by then he was already communicating with half a dozen of them, so he had one foot out the door and no motivation to work on the marriage. I know he turned to those women because it was easier to get praise from them than to work on himself in our relationship, so they were an outcome of his feelings rather than the instigator of the marriage breakdown."

"From where I stand now, in a different relationship, I can also see the areas where my ex insisted I needed to improve, which I resisted. With my new partner, I've had to train myself to be less critical and to give him more space and choice about fulfilling my needs in a way that works for both of us. My ex used to say, 'you need to give me some room to work,' and it was jarring when my new partner had the same complaint, though he didn't express it in the same words. It's hard to envision how I could have done it much differently with my ex, though. There were so many areas where I stayed quiet or made the choice I knew he would prefer, so I kind of feel like, when I asked for a specific change from him, he should have tried to honor it. But I don't know."

"We stopped being kind to each other."

"We were too young and immature to accept the responsibilities of marriage and children. Our backgrounds were different; so were our goals and ambitions. It was also a different time (1950s)."

"I think we were both too young and immature to focus on the relationship. Every problem thus became one that drove the wedge deeper."

"It was sort of doomed from the start."

"We got married way too young—it was real love. We thought we were mature enough to get married and face life. Reality set in years later when I saw my friends with responsibilities."

"Money problems, his not including family in decisions, a sick child, an online pornography addiction that got him fired, lying, us not talking honestly with each other, and me pleading with him to talk. It was bad."

"He didn't try to meet me even halfway for what I needed in the relationship."

"He was a grade-A asshole who had no idea what a healthy relationship, much less a marriage, should look like. He was clueless about how to pitch in around the house other than mowing, rarely helped me do anything, and was awful in the bedroom. Just ick all around."

"I am codependent and allowed my husband to manipulate me into thinking I am the cause of his anger issues."

Emotional health should be a priority. If not, it can exact a toll on the relationship.

"He was struggling with depression and anxiety and didn't get help to manage it, just leaned on me. I felt helpless because I couldn't make him feel better and began to feel like there was no room for 'me' in the relationship. The me that was there was objectionable and inadequate."

"Untreated mental illness."

"His mental health."

"My illness was scary. The meds utterly changed me. My inability to see that I was sinking in a spiral of irrational thinking due to the medicine's side effects which made my bipolar condition much worse. If I could, *I* would have left me."

"I finally got the courage to leave when I adopted a dog. (He previously wouldn't let me have one.)"

"He wanted to be a cult leader and thought the world was going to end and refused to work and spent all day online. And when I asked for a divorce, he 'forbade' me from seeking one."

Bad behaviors can also be abusive. (If people grow up accustomed to being mistreated, they may not realize how bad it is at first.)

"He physically, mentally, and sexually abused me and my kids."

"Entitlement and abuse."

"The final straw was that she overtly tried to alienate me from my family. She had already separated me from my friend group and hobbies. I was only allowed to do the things she wanted, with her friends and family. She also hit me on several occasions, once breaking my nose. She blamed me for her abusive behavior and used guilt and other passive-aggressive tactics to get her way if I tried to resist. The week before she told me she wanted a divorce, she took me on a trip to spend a week with her family, which was horrible (I think she had already told them). I asked to try counseling, and in our session, she told me that if I didn't stop spending time with my (recently widowed) mom, that it was over. I was unwilling to accept that, so we started working on separation."

"His verbal and emotional abuse."

"In the end, it became toxic. I ended it because of verbal and emotional abuse, but in fairness to him, I'm the one who taught him and allowed him, from the beginning of our relationship, to treat me in a way that was often demeaning, condescending, and not a partnership. When I finally stood up for myself, he didn't understand why there was a problem, since I'd never pushed back before. He would say, 'these aren't real issues, this is marriage.'"

"He was verbally and emotionally abusive. I cheated a lot, compulsively. I realized what was wrong with me and did not feel confident to address it within the marriage or put him through that. We did also have very different goals and approaches to life, but we might have been able to get through that."

"Emotional and verbal abuse."

Addiction can cause or contribute to mistreatment.

"Alcohol was his best friend and made him even more of a nasty person."

"No question: our marriage ended due to my ex's alcohol dependence and polysubstance addictions, which remain untreated. My legal separation happened due to my spouse's alcohol dependence and his emotional derision, undermining the trust of my son. This culminated in my son (a young adult who had the power of independence) deciding not to come home anymore once he saw that my husband was not going to acknowledge or repair the harm done as he lost a second father to addictions. Once my son said he would not be coming home again—ever—I was gone in under a month."

Communication issues or incompatibility can widen the distance between couples.

"In hindsight, we were terrible at communicating. We both shied from conflict and would avoid dealing with difficult topics. There were many needs in the relationship that were not being met."

"I don't think I led the relationship very well. I allowed myself to base decisions off of her emotions and they changed with the wind. I was not the constant force or stability in the emotional storm. I attempted to be nimble and accepting, and ignored many things in my wife."

"We had fundamentally different communication styles: I ask lots of questions; she hated being asked questions. I wanted my partner to ask me lots of questions; she didn't like to do that. We also grew apart politically."

"His emotional inaccessibility when I needed more emotional support during a long-term family crisis [were an issue]."

A lack of intimacy might contribute to a weakening bond.

"We simply grew apart. We were very different in all aspects. We were more friends. There was no romantic attraction."

"We were more like good friends engaged in the business of raising kids, than lovers. This truth was reflected in a lack of defense or public support from her when her family openly attacked me at gatherings. There were also years of virtually no physical intimacy between us."

"There was an age difference, and it became more like living with my father than my husband. Lack of intimacy. We slept in separate beds."

"My wife came home one day and said, 'I'm thinking of leaving you.' (I thought I was in a happy marriage.) Six weeks later she moved out. Marriage counseling failed, and we got divorced."

"The physical part was not satisfying to either of us. We kind of turned into just roommates who got along well and that was it."

"It was the classic 'We grew apart' situation. I began to really resent him, and vice versa. I struggled with bipolar disorder (he had it too—we met in a support group), and over time, I felt like he labeled me as 'the sick wife.' I felt limited, and knew if I were ever to get better for the long run, I had to get out from under his assessment of me. So sad, really. I had felt like when we married I was 'broken' and he accepted that and loved me despite myself. As I grew older I regretted that I settled for marrying him because I didn't think anyone else would. SAD."

"I felt lonely and trapped."

"Our physical/sexual relationship was nonexistent/dormant for years at a stretch, but I see that as much as a consequence of other things than as a cause."

Infidelity is often a sign of other issues.

"A story as old as time: infidelity, fueled by what I was positive was *anything* but a subconscious desire to sabotage and thus end my marriage. It turns out it was *entirely* a subconscious desire to sabotage and thus end my marriage. Could have saved several people, including myself, a LOT of pain had I figured that out sooner. Sigh."

"We grew apart, she cheated, I walked away."

"[One sign was] going outside of marriage to solve issues instead of dealing with them together."

"He was having an affair."

"Incompatibility compounded by betrayal."

"He decided I wasn't the kind of wife he needed in his life. He cheated."

"I was desperately lonely and had felt so small for so long that having another person appreciate me unmoored me. What I should have done is gone straight to counseling when the feelings started to arise."

"Multiple infidelities."

Mismatches or changes in sexuality or intimacy can impact the connection.

"I could no longer ignore our deeply mismatched physical chemistry."

"It is hard for a relationship to have equilibrium when one person is homosexual and one person is heterosexual. Leaving helped me obtain equilibrium."

"It was increasingly difficult to be intimate in the bedroom because I felt his contempt and frustration outside of it. Even little things, like making fun of my tastes in music or art, ended up making me feel small. There is no greater libido-killer than crushing confidence and self-worth."

"He was transgender before it was a thing and came out to me. I wasn't interested in that. I wanted a man. It ended."

"They had fetishes I did not share."

"Before you go, would you mind taking a few moments to fill out a short form rating your relationship experience?"

Chapter 6

Does your ex agree with you on why things ended? If not, what did they say were the reasons?

If they agreed:

"Yes. He knows he was mainly at fault for the demise of our marriage not only due to his affair but also other behaviors like stonewalling, lying, being financially irresponsible, blaming me for everything, etc."

"I think we were mostly on the same page as to why things ended."

"Yes, and she has said that at the time, it was difficult for her to look inside herself, and thus, share herself with me."

"He would say I destroyed his world. And with no warning. He would not have wanted to divorce me. But he can see how it happened over time and how I felt."

"We agree that we were too young but we have no regrets. It took a while but we remained friends."

"Yes. It was very white and black."

"I think she would agree with me. She acknowledged her criticism, contempt, and defensiveness in our last-ditch couples therapy sessions and in a post-separation letter of apology/expression of regret that she wrote to me. We would both agree that my affair was the final/fatal blow. We would both agree that our communication styles did not mesh."

"Yes, he did. He owned responsibility, but I was unwilling to give any more chances."

If it's a gray area:

"Some things yes and some no. He tended to consider himself generally blameless in all things, and it's very hard to have a relationship with a person like that."

"He doesn't deny what he did but, based on our last conversations, I think he believes that what he did was a fair reaction to my having certain physical issues. He blames me."

"I think we'd agree on why things ended. I'm not sure I'll ever know how much she's come to terms with what was wrong beyond the mere fact of infidelity."

"I'm not sure he truly believed it. His feeling was that it was 'all your fault.' After each separation we worked at it for about two months, but that's not enough to have a good marriage (notice I didn't say happy)."

If they do not agree:

"He tells people it ended because I didn't want to take care of him anymore and that I was lying about the rage outbursts and the abusive behaviors and that the infidelities didn't count or matter because he said he was sorry (and not everybody even knows about that part). He's actively still campaigning against me and vilifying me."

"No, he would say he was unhappy."

"No, the ex gaslit her friends (as she gaslit me during the marriage) to make me the bad guy. All of the abuse she carried out in the marriage, she projected onto her version of me and presented that to those who would listen to her."

"No. He did not see what he did wrong. I never told him I cheated, though I'm pretty sure he knew."

"No, he would say we just argued and that I trigger him."

"No, he says it's all my fault that I promised to change and do better and never did. He always said everything was my fault."

"We exited each other's life hurt, covered with a veil of strength to show we were good without each other. We've not had a deep conversation on why things ended. I had to learn words and tools to express what it was that I was feeling, and that didn't come until after things ended."

"The divorce was amicable."

"Of course I disagree, and this does not even scratch the surface, but at our last counseling session he admitted he was angry because I 'had lied to him when he met me' about how much money I would be making in my career. Most of the fights in our late marriage were about money. We were middle class and he wanted to be wealthy. He felt that as he was already at the top of his (librarian) earning potential, it was up to me to make up the difference, and my failure to do so was a betrayal."

"No, she does not. To absolve herself from her having to look inward and acknowledge her own contributions to the deteriorating dynamic that lead to the demise of our relationship, she has fashioned a story that I was a philanderer with a secret life who left her out of the blue and she was a woman scorned."

"He never saw any reason to end the relationship. He was content."

"No, he thinks it was to be with someone new."

"No, he doesn't. Shortly after we separated I started dating someone and he will always contend that the marriage ended because I met someone else."

"No, he doesn't realize how horrible he was."

"No. He tells everyone (including our kids) that I cheated on him. Truth is, when alcohol takes a hold of someone, the other person can relish in just a decent conversation with a person of the opposite sex and find a modicum of happiness. So it came close to happening but never did."

"No, he would say I was too controlling."

"I doubt it . . . she thought she was justified to do the things she did. Three weeks after the divorce was finalized, she tried to break into my house to see what I was doing . . . she brought people to help her force her way and break in."

"We both agreed she was unhappy. We disagreed (at the time) on the source of her unhappiness (me and the marriage). I don't know any more. We've had no contact in 12 years."

"His constant claim was that 'you think everything is my fault, I'm the bad guy, I just do everything wrong.' He felt that very strongly, but I really don't know how you compromise or meet halfway about something like your partner telling you he never wants to hear you talk about your job again. I feel like that's objectively just a very shitty thing for him to say. Maybe you can compromise about how much you talk about it, but you have to start from a point where they retract that statement and apologize for making it. Or how he said he would have sex with me more if I did the dishes more. What do you do with a statement like that? He would say these types of things and then double down on them when they came up in marriage counseling, so it wasn't just a 'heat of anger' thing."

"No, he felt he was doing everything I needed."

Some weren't sure.

"Nope. I have no idea, we never speak."

"I have no idea. She won't talk to me anymore."

"I have no idea. We don't speak."

"I don't know what his explanations are, but it ended because I decided to end it."

"I think she would agree; I am not sure, though."

"My ex will not speak to me. He is also very repressed. One of my two children still speaks to him, and she gets frustrated with his lack of ability to empathize. I am not sure I will ever know. He just repeats the same talking points over and over again with my daughter, so it is hard to know what he thinks. He does not respond until his wife tells him what to say. My daughter gets very upset by it."

"My ex-husband sometimes agrees with me on why things ended but more often lapses into a mindset that I left for no reason at all. My separated spouse takes no responsibility for his alcohol addiction and talks as if I left him for no discernible reason, and that my son dislikes him with no cause."

"Never underestimate the power of denial."

"Hell if I know. I never spoke to him again after I packed up and moved out prior to filing."

"You know, all these years later I am having trouble remembering why he thought the marriage ended. He likely would have said it was my being bipolar. I am sure it was hard to live with me at times. My depressions were debilitating, although I never ended up in a mental ward. I was treated outpatient and that remains true today."

"At the time, he was confused. I'm not sure what he thought as time went by and he processed further. We haven't spoken in a decade."

"I'm not sure. I think she'd say it was the infidelity."

"He wanted the marriage to end and was passive-aggressive. He was mean and abusive. He found a way in his mind to rationalize his actions."

"BEING MARRIED TO HER WAS THE MOST MISERABLE EXPERIENCE OF MY LIFE, BUT I WAS ABLE TO DEVELOP A SITCOM OUT OF IT."

Chapter 7

What is positive about where you are now (post-divorce or separation)?

"A smooth sea never made a skilled sailor."
~Franklin D. Roosevelt

The ending of a relationship that isn't working can create space for a better match.

"I'm happily re-coupled, in a challenging but infinitely rewarding relationship built on mutual respect, shared values, honest communication, and buzzy physical attraction. Thanks in large part to financial assistance from a parent, I emerged from divorce financially whole—with the house, relatively little debt, and excellent credit. (I am endlessly grateful and lucky.)"

"I am remarried and believe this marriage is much healthier and ultimately happier."

"I am now in my second marriage that, despite having its flaws too, is neither verbally nor physically abusive, and he listens more and helps out more than first hubby. New husband and I have been together five times as long as first husband and I were. I have a daughter now (not biologically his; sperm donor), and he is a pretty good dad, although his temper is short. Sure, it could be better, but I'm doing so much better in this relationship than the last one. New hubby is funny and we do have some really good moments."

"I'm in a much healthier relationship and I know myself so much better. I have a sense of inner peace I've never had before. I now understand what I need, how I want to be treated, how to read people better, and how to communicate well. My current partner and I never fight. We talk all the time about difficult things but we don't need to yell about them. There is no power struggle. I feel cherished and revered in the ways I've always needed."

"I'm remarried, with kids and in a different city and different career (stay-at-home dad) that I never imagined for myself. My life is so different than before!"

"I'm in an amazing marriage this time around. My husband was left by his wife, also against his will. He is committed to marriage and to me and it's amazing! I'm grateful for the twisty journey that got me here."

"I am in a peaceful relationship where no one has any mental illness or abusive tendencies."

"Finally healed my childhood wound of seeking validation externally, looking for outside approval."

"I'm with a much more compatible partner and I have been able to be more myself."

"Oh my god . . . so much positive. I have found my match in love and life, despite the hardships we face. My husband has a heart of gold, treats people with love and respect, and he is everything I deserve and need in this life. He loves my family and doesn't resent any time given to others. We are each other's partner. It's an amazing revelation. While life is still hard for so many reasons (family drama, finances, health, etc.), we both feel like having one another makes it easier. <3"

It can be hard to turn an unhappy marriage around, but happiness doesn't have to be out of reach forever.

"I love where I am now ... now I'm in a fantastic relationship (of 3+ years) and we just purchased a home together (first home for me). I have opened my own business since then, among many other accomplishments along the way. I also went through a very transformative period, with the help of therapy, to work through emotional abuse that I suffered during my marriage. I'm so much happier now!"

"We are both happier people."

"I am happy to not be in that relationship any longer."

"There's a ton that's very positive about where I am now. I love my new career, which I only started training for after I was separated. I'm in a relationship that is much more respectful and with much better communication, and with a much better human being, too. As a result of that, I have learned better relationship communication skills and I feel much more loved. I feel good about how I have maintained things—my house, my relationships with my kids, my life in general. Honestly, I also really like having this much authority over my space and my life. I miss having an intact family, but I don't personally miss my ex at all. I really like the degree to which my life feels like my own."

"I am unencumbered by emotional dead-weights I used to carry."

"I love having freedom and independence, financially and socially. My ex and I remain good friends and the co-parenting experience has gone so well, I don't know how it could really be better. We are both doing really well in our careers and are financially stable, too. I am happy to have had the experience of being married to a good person for five years, and also to have had the experience of a divorce that was amicable. I don't have any regrets at all. Another good thing is that my ex remarried a wonderful woman, which helped assuage any lingering guilt I might have felt about initiating the split from him—it makes me really happy to see him happy and flourishing, and his wife is super cool and an amazing stepmom to my daughter as well."

"I love my new home, my freedom, and the relationship I have with my now-adult son. I am proud of what I've been able to build in my personal and professional life, and of my resilience. I feel satisfaction and achievement in my growing abilities to do many things I had never tried to accomplish before. I've learned to install floors, wire ceiling fans, change headlamps, and insulate attics, and I am proud of me. I also had serious doubts about whether I could support my own household . . . my separated spouse had made me feel that maybe I could not do it. Turns out, I can."

Personal growth is always a good thing.

"My only regret was not getting divorced earlier. Looking back, I was so unhappy for so many years."

"Therapy. Lots and lots of therapy, ongoing for the last six years for me and the kids. I am married, which is a total surprise."

"After our divorce, I realized that I was not mature enough to have gotten married and therefore my expectations probably led to some of the problems. Accepting your part in the final break is a great healer. It also allows you to admit that you did love this person and always will, just not as a life partner."

"Starting to be [positive]. Bought my own home, which was HUGE. My kids have grown into really nice adults."

"At least I don't have to grind through year after year of struggling to make the marriage work."

"I feel comfortable in my own skin. I have learned I AM okay being alone. And I'm a role model to my daughter about how to stand up for yourself, move on after adversity, and find your own happiness."

"I became reacquainted with a good friend from college who was going through a similar situation. We are now married and have a son . . . life is so much better."

"I learned a lot about myself, made new friends, had wonderful adventures, and met my husband of now 18 years."

"I am now aware of my strength and resilience. I have learned so many life lessons about boundary setting, understanding my own expectations in any relationship, breaking out of codependency."

"I have financial stability, a quiet, stable household. And a very happy daughter."

"I'm still on this journey. I can appreciate that we are in control of our own happiness and never place or accept the burden of making someone else happy."

"I learned that I was stronger than I gave myself credit for and got both kids through high school on only a $24K-a-year salary. I also paid off all debts incurred before the divorce in two and a half years. I have a terrific relationship with my children!"

"I know a lot about myself and accept more about myself now than I did then."

"I am so much happier. I love not being criticized all the time. I love not having to listen to my ex-wife. I love being able to keep my house neat and organized. I enjoy being able to cook (my ex had been very controlling in the kitchen). I am enjoying being able to explore sexual fantasies with my girlfriend."

"I am happy, I feel I am my own person. And find peace getting to know myself."

"I had the chance to travel and experience life. I am more open-minded and can rely on myself."

"I no longer 'need' someone to survive. Of course, I need people, but I am self-sufficient and any person coming into my life would be a complement to it. I have also addressed the emotional scarring behind the compulsive cheating, so I have a much more honest, transparent, healthy approach to partnership."

"I believe in myself now. I didn't when I was married to my first husband."

"I accept that you can't get back to that place you once knew. I learned more about myself than I knew was possible. I never lost the memories. I learned to accept rather than regret life. 'For better or worse' says it all."

"I'm out from awful, terrifying relationships. I'm safe. My kids are safe. There's no yelling. There's no wondering what will happen next, what the day will bring, in a fearful way. I can come and go as I please. It's blissful to just be safe."

"I'm not dead yet. I have realized that even though my time with her was brief, it was the best three years of my life, being with her. I now know that being alone does not mean feeling lonely. I still try to look at each day with hope that this world will do better and maybe I can help that along."

"Once he remarried, life got easier—he was no longer stalking me. I still had to interact with him concerning the kids, and that was always unpleasant."

Parents and kids can grow closer as change fosters growth.

"The relationship with my daughter is strong."

"My kids and I enjoy much more open communication and have a better relationship and dynamic together than when my (former) wife was with us. I am healthier both mentally and physically."

"I am free, my children are strong and healthy."

"My relationship with my kids, though not without bumps along the way, has been strong; I wound up with a very favorable custody arrangement and have been able to remain integral to their lives as they enter adulthood. Again: endlessly grateful and lucky."

"My ex and I get along and have worked together in the best interest of the kids. I am close with my kids, who are all emotionally healthy and resilient. I'm happily remarried. I have recovered financially. I'm very happy and very thankful."

"We never speak poorly of the other to our daughter, and we make shared decisions about her. And share the cost."

"[We are] completely on the same page with decisions about our child. We are able to be civil with each other, and he doesn't give me a hard time about paying for stuff she needs."

"And another thing. I don't want you visiting my Web site."

Chapter 8

What is difficult about where you are now (post-divorce or separation)?

Sometimes the past complicates the present.

"The hardest part is that we both have baggage from our previous marriages. It gets in our way sometimes."

"[Challenging] blended family dynamics, as I am remarried now."

"Family dramas with kids, financial stress, COVID, job security, the lack of ability to retire in our future, the medical needs in our future we are unsure of …"

"The inability to share family stories and memories and lore."

"My ex still refuses to accept his part in the marriage failing. When alcohol is involved and you're in denial, it can make things spiral out of control. It takes two to make a marriage work, but it can also take two to make it crumble and fail. Both parties have to accept their part."

Lingering aftermath on kids.

"[I have] guilt about how hurt my children are. [Also] the neverending effort to not treat my current partner like they have the same behaviors as my ex."

"My relationship with my ex is essentially nonexistent, and that places a strain on the kids, who get stuck acting as go-betweens. There is no co-parenting, and she provides little to no financial assistance—again, fine with me, but not so great for the kids."

"I feel very bad about my kids' relationship with their father."

"My 11-year-old son sees me as the bad guy and his dad as the good guy. He thinks I take too much money from his dad, which makes his dad poor. He also believes that I am trying to keep him from his dad. All of these things are so far from the truth it's laughable. His dad plays the victim in his own life and complains to my son. His dad is unemployed, yet again, not due to COVID, but due to getting fired. I wish my son knew how distorted his father is."

"I still have to deal with the exes because there are children involved."

"My son was also hurt in the divorce and he will not permit any contact from his abusive mother."

"Worrying about my kids. Wishing I could do it over for them knowing what I know now. I wish I could give them a happy childhood. I am a much better mom now than I was when I was when we were in the thick of it, and they know I will always have their backs. It's okay, though."

"My ex-husband threatened to abuse me while he was under the influence. He blacked out and did not remember it later, but our son saw it all and remembers every detail. Our son has refused to see, write, or speak to his father since that time, seven years ago. It's hard to see my son pining for and working through forgiving his father while refusing to communicate with him at any level, but I understand his choice and I support it. I admire his strength, and I mourn that it's necessary."

"The biggest difficulty is my relationship with my daughter, although to be fair, the problems with her began before the divorce."

"When it comes to the kids, it feels like I lost some time. When you share custody with kids, you lose time with them. You miss stuff. I did the best I could [with] showing up, but as they get older you wish you could hit rewind sometimes and see more of the moments you missed."

New or different challenges with co-parenting (or parenting alone).

"[It's hard] that he has a new relationship with someone much younger while I deal with all the day-to-day parenting."

"He can still be a giant ass on the rare occasions he feels inconvenienced by caring for her. This is becoming irrelevant as she is near to aging out of custody."

Emotional repercussions can linger.

"I lack self-confidence and question everything."

"I question my judgment when it comes to relationships— how could I have gotten it so wrong the first time? I use my family and friends as a gut-check if I meet someone new that

I'm interested in dating."

"I have a hard time with the difference between what I expected and how I've failed. I've tried and failed at marriage again. It's hard to do that after working so hard to make this marriage work."

"My self-esteem has taken a hit even though I know logically that there's no working things out with a person with active, untreated addictions. It's hard to see that I chose two men with addictions and not think it's me. It's hard to think that others may see me as a failure in this important area of my life."

"I still don't feel great about this part of my past. I wanted a union that lasted forever."

"I'm also still getting used to some ways in which my new relationship is different from my old one. It's hard to accept that you can't 'have it all' in a single relationship, especially when you view it as an 'upgrade.' My ex might have been an asshole in many ways, but he was an asshole who was very adventurous, great at traveling, and full of ideas and energy for weekend excursions. My new partner is not like that. And that's one thing I really miss. But the bottom line is that I can go to Vegas by myself, but I can't sit down with myself in the evening and talk to myself about my day. And that's something my partner is really, really good at—listening, remembering details, truly wanting that time and opportunity to connect with me. So I can accept the loss of that type of excitement in my relationship, but it can still frustrate me, and then it further frustrates me that I'm frustrated with it, because it feels too close to missing my ex, which I know isn't actually the case."

"Marriage and family require personal growth and humility. Those things are a challenge and easy to fall out of."

"I'm still a broken person. But that isn't a result of the divorce. It was true to begin with."

"I still have anxiety from behaviors that remind me of the mental part of [my ex's] abuse. My wife is also a victim of abuse who shuts down to avoid any conflict . . . this used to cause us trouble, but we've worked on learning to communicate better . . . I feel more secure in our relationship when she needs space to think and she feels more willing to share her negative feelings rather than bottling them up."

"I'm wondering if I want to move on into another adult relationship. I can take the time I need to think about that. But it's not a choice I had imagined contemplating."

"[I am] unwilling to enter into another relationship."

"Finding that yet another husband preferred alcohol to marriage with me changed my feelings toward my spouse quite a lot. I don't miss living with him at all. I don't miss our intimate/sexual life. I vastly enjoy sleeping alone and making all my own choices. I love him like people love family, not like I love a lover. It's a sense of familial love, not the love I want to feel for a mate."

Financial difficulties can also persist.

"The only difficulty is financially. It's easier to have a two-income household."

"Money, always."

"Lingering financial difficulties."

"Finances, primarily. I feel stressed about money and how I will make enough of it."

"Financially, it is hard to support a home and pay alimony."

"I am not sure if I will be able to buy the kind of house I want in the kind of neighborhood I want, but I am actually very happy renting, at least for now. Since I still live in the same town as my ex, I don't feel entirely comfortable walking around town, but I am no longer hiding either."

"The lost financial and emotional ground was significant."

"Starting over buying a home was so much harder. We likely would have had the mortgage paid off by now, but I'm living in a place half the size with $200K left to pay off even a decade later."

"Financially, [I'm] so much worse off. Military guys make bank when deployed: hazard pay, housing allowance, great health care, tax-free shopping on base, lots of support systems, etc. My in-laws in the first marriage were SAINTS! They helped us and me out so much. Just the sweetest people."

It's not uncommon to miss your ex or mourn the life you once had.

"I still attempt to find understanding in why things ended instead of just accepting that the relationship ended. I have to remind myself that there are things I can work on, and I'm down to do the work, but she left and I [must] accept her decision."

"Sometimes seeing a picture of her can hurt. A sharp ache on the inside. It's like being reminded of a limb that I lost."

"I miss his constant friendship. Once either of us has another partner, we will have to lose a lot of our connection. Already we are both preparing for this, calling and seeing each other less and no longer saying 'I love you.'"

"I miss the good times we shared as a family unit and the promise that held."

"It's hard to let go of the thousand gossamer strands that tied my separated spouse and me together. There are dozens of tiny reminders of what we've lost. Social media reminds us of this or that event we hosted, or the day we both drove my son to his first college dorm room. Or the neighborhood camping trips that we took. It's working through losses on many levels. Grief is hard."

Loneliness is also common.

"Still working out the new normals. Wishing for a kind relationship with a partner."

"I don't have anyone to functionally/practically lean on during difficult situations, so I've had to reduce my adventurousness with new things."

"Ten years post-divorce, I don't currently have a partner, and I am not too hopeful about that changing. So that is a little lonely sometimes, but I try to count my blessings, of which I have plenty, and remember that being married or in a relationship could be lonely sometimes too."

"I had to leave our circle of friends behind, but they were all too small-minded to allow me to fit into their world view."

"Loneliness."

"No partner. With aging, it seems too many 'available' potential partners don't take care of themselves psychologically or physically, and/or have not sorted through their personal issues. I prefer to be alone rather than deal with a woman who isn't cultivating her best self."

"It sucks to be alone sometimes! I appreciate alone time and downtime, but I do miss being in an intimate, significant relationship."

"There's a lot less sex in my current marriage/life. I feel old. I don't know if that's a result of the divorce/new partner or just because I'm older, and that might have happened anyway."

With time comes more peace.

"Nothing, all positive."

"Our kids are adults now, so I don't need to deal with him very often, but there will always be the occasional interaction."

"My now-husband and I very rarely have sex, because of his physical health issues. And yet I feel so loved. I'm staying!"

"Nothing is difficult other than knowing there are fewer years ahead of me than behind."

"I'm hoping to buy back everything I lost in the divorce at the garage sale she's having."

CartoonStock.com

Chapter 9

Are you hopeful about the future?

Yes:

"Yes, very much so! I really do feel like my ex did me a huge favor by leaving me. He didn't do the kids a huge favor by any stretch, but me personally, yes he did. I feel like the best thing he ever did for me was marry me and the second-best thing was leave me. We had outgrown each other, and his choice to leave freed me up, in my forties, to have the life I would actually freely choose. I'm no longer confined by the choices I made when I was 20 years old. And I love the possibilities that lie ahead for me, and it feels exciting to be able to direct my future based on my own preferences."

"Absolutely."

"Yes. I have the rest of my life to live. It's mine."

"I'd like to offer a bit of advice to anyone facing divorce. Divorce is impossibly hard and it brings out the worst in us. Just remember that you have to pick up the pieces when it's done. You have to live with YOU when it's done. Don't do or say anything that future you will regret. I imagined myself 10 years down the road and asked, 'Will I regret saying this? Will I regret not doing this? Will I even care about this?' Run everything by future you. This helped me have very few things I regret now (at least of the things I could control)."

"Most days, yes."

"As much as the world feels like an exploding heap of soiled diapers, my own life is full of cause for hope: I'm in the right relationship, I waited the right amount of time between divorce and new commitment (and thus banked a lot of happy memories during single life), and I'm excited for new adventures as the kids head out into the world. Divorce is the absolute worst, but it ends."

"I'm excited that I got out of the fruitless marriage early and can refocus my energy on me and what/who adds value to what I've built. I'm looking for a different kind of woman than I did when I first met my ex. I'm also at a different point in my life… I intend to enjoy my current situation."

"Yes!!"

"Sure, the severance from the toxic behaviors is complete. I am surrounded now by a peaceful family."

"Yes, 100%."

"Very! No matter what happens, I know my husband is

committed to me for life. We have seen the worst that life and marriage have to offer and we both want to fight for the best. Together."

"Yes. Hopeful and happy."

"Yes. One child has moved out already, the other will also be on his own eventually, and we will feel a bit more 'free' from drama."

"I'm more hopeful now after my freedom."

"Yes! I feel like I have a lot of happy things still to look forward to—my daughter growing up, me growing old with family and friends, a world to explore through travel and learning, creative projects, and so on. I can't wait to be retired and have more time to relax and have fun adventures."

"I'm hopeful about my life in general. I've been separated for over five months now, and there aren't ever enough hours in the day for all I want to achieve. Life is exciting, and I feel more productive than ever before. When I lived with my separated spouse, I spent a lot of time waiting on/around/for him. Now the liberation is inspiring."

"YES!! The future is bright!"

"Yes. Hope is what you have when you realize that your attitude affects your reality. It's not the cards you are dealt, it's how you play them."

"Absolutely! I'm two years newly married to a wonderful man!!"

"Remember that God is as good in the dark as He is in the light. You will feel alone and abandoned but that doesn't mean you are. Trust that He is there whether you feel Him or not. Hold tight and remind yourself that this is only a phase. If you try to hold onto your grace and patience and faithfulness, you'll come out of this stronger and more beautiful."

"Very. I am in a much better place. We just celebrated our tenth anniversary. I have a partner who supports me in my aspirations, and lets me support her in hers. We have common friends that we made together, and that one or the other of us brought into the relationship. Communication is a thing."

"Yes, [although there are] new challenges—children issues!"

"For my own personal life, yes. For the fate of humanity, no."

"Future is good. I'm 10 years past those events."

"In general, yes."

"In many ways, yes. I know that I can make of my life what I want. That is, I took control of my life and acted. I will be fine financially. I worry a lot about my relationship with my daughter, and I wonder what my life will look like in a decade or two (I'm currently 54), but three years after I moved out, and one year after the divorce was finalized, I'm doing well."

"Yes, I look forward to meeting someone and continuing my growth and healing."

"I am [hopeful], because I'm not hinging my hope or happiness on the existence or absence of a relationship. I am growing as a human being and that's my focus."

"Yes, because my now-husband supports me emotionally and spiritually. I look forward to growing old with him. Every day we find something to laugh about and enjoy!"

"Yes, I am hopeful."

"Absolutely!"

"Positively! I have a wonderful family. I'm looking forward to many more productive years."

"I believe with good fortune I will have a strong marriage and a loving family for many years to come."

"Have to be!"

"I wouldn't want to go through divorce again, but I will say that it does force you to grow in many ways. You can use the experience to become stronger, wiser, and more self-aware."

"Yes, but my divorce was over 40 years ago."

No:

"No. But that is due to the political climate and coronavirus."

"Eh, not really. I still struggle to make ends meet. We live hand to mouth. [My second husband's] temper is short, he yells a lot, his personal hygiene is lacking, he's not that cute anymore (older, fatter, balder, smellier), he neglects his appearance and health, etc. We haven't had any intimacy in five years (no kissing or hugging, rare holding hands, usually for safety issues), and no sex. I tolerate him most of the time, but he annoys me a lot. If I could afford to leave him and never marry again, I probably would."

Not sure:

"I doubt we can ever be friends, which makes me sad, but at least we can get along. I probably will not see or hear much of him after she turns 18."

"Not really."

"I can answer that on Election Day."

"Regarding hope about another future partnership: it depends on the day. I spent a dozen years with the man I'm now legally separated from. He either developed alcohol addiction seven years into our marriage, or (more probably) he had the issues the whole time but hid them for the first seven years. Whichever is true, this has opened up many old wounds and I find myself questioning whether I would ever get involved in another relationship or marriage again. I wonder whether I can trust my own judgment and whether it's worth taking another chance. I feel like I've built such a good life without a partner that perhaps I won't do more than date. On the other hand, I am good at loving. Maybe not great at picking, but good at loving. And it would be a shame to let these past experiences deprive me of loving again."

"Time will tell."

"I'm hopeful for a good life, but don't have a lot of hope to find someone I'd want to be with."

· · ·
Part 2

Practical Advice and Guidance

· · ·

Chapter 10

Should I stay or should I go? How do I figure that out?

Counseling can help (together and individually), but if you're looking for a good book while waiting for your first appointment, I recommend *Too Good to Leave, Too Bad to Stay: A Step-by-Step Guide to Help You Decide Whether to Stay In or Get Out of Your Relationship* by Mira Kirshenbaum.

She describes over 30 factors that help people consider which issues may respond to help and which will likely not improve no matter how much time and energy is thrown at them. It can help knowing which is which if you're on the fence.

ABUSE WARNING

If your relationship is abusive, do NOT go to couples counseling.

Abuse is not a relationship problem.

Counseling helps couples understand each other and gain perspective.

It cannot fix the uneven power structure characteristic of an abusive relationship.

Learn more at https://www.thehotline.org/identify-abuse/power-and-control or call the National Domestic Violence Hotline at 1-800-799-SAFE (7233) or call 211.

How to find the right therapist

If you try couples therapy, look for someone who specializes in either of the following methods, as there is evidence they are more effective:

• Gottman Method

☐ The weekend workshops called *The Art and Science of Love* have been shown to achieve results similar to those of six months of marital therapy. https://www.gottman.com/couples/workshops/art-science-of-love

(Note: workshops alone are insufficient for the 20%–30% of couples who have deeper issues such as a history of infidelity or depression; these can be addressed only in therapy.)

☐ Wondering what a workshop is like? Read what one couple wrote about their experience: https://goop.com/wellness/relationships/gottman-institute-couples-workshop

☐ History and overview of Gottman research: https://hellorelish.com/articles/gottman-method-overview-history.html

☐ Gottman Method under the microscope: https://www.psychotherapynetworker.org/blog/details/430/the-gottman-method-couples-therapy-under-the-microscope

• Emotionally Focused Therapy (EFT)

☐ An Emotionally Focused Therapy (EFT) study found that after 8 to 12 sessions, a majority of couples had healed their injuries and rebuilt their trust, and these gains lasted at least three years: https://www.nytimes.com/2005/04/19/health/psychology/married-with-problems-therapy-may-not-help.html

If your partner isn't on board, then seeing a counselor on your own can be extremely valuable.

People often worry that counseling won't help. But it can be immensely powerful *even if your partner will not attend*. Therapy offers tools to cope and to learn how to behave in such a way that you can bring out the best in yourself and your mate.

While some of the effectiveness of couples counseling depends on how safe and comfortable you both feel with the counselor, the methodology is also important. Don't feel shy asking about their work—therapists are used to being questioned about how they help people. It's okay to research and interview potential counselors before hiring them.

Misconceptions about therapy:

- It's okay to guide your sessions and ask for what you need out of them. You are the expert on what it's like to be in your skin and it's okay to match the level of support to your needs. Sometimes insurance covers multiple visits a week.

- It's okay to see more than one therapist.

- Don't be ashamed to change counselors if it doesn't feel like the right fit. Therapists understand and appreciate when their clients advocate for themselves. Their feelings will not be hurt if you part ways.

- You don't necessarily need to dive into your entire background first—you can just start where you are.

If there is a history of trauma for either you or your partner, make sure the therapist uses a "**trauma-informed**" approach, meaning that they understand the myriad ways a history of trauma can affect individuals and couples.

How do I end things? I'm not sure where to start.

If you've come to the realization that this is the end, expressing this is often the hardest part of the entire separation process. It can be difficult to know what to say, when, or how, especially if you're ambivalent. Maybe things would work if only changes could stick? Or maybe it's become clear that the relationship isn't working. Initiating this first conversation can be brutal.

These types of conversations seem to fall into one of two categories:

1. **The danger zone:** The relationship is in danger. There's still hope, but only if fundamental changes are made *and kept*. These changes may be internal or external (or both), and individual or couples therapy may help.

2. **The end zone:** The relationship is over for at least one partner. If at least one partner feels it's past the point of no return, therapy may be useful for the separation process but not usually for a repair. If you're delivering the news, it's better not to go into great detail because reasons are often seen as negotiable.

If you're initiating an "ending" conversation, keep in mind your partner's needs. They'll want to know:

- What does this mean about your future relationship?

- How will things be after you separate?

- Will you stay friends or be friendly?

- How will money be handled?

- What will the new living situation be? Where will each of you be living?

What you both need most is to know, "Do you still have my back?" Talking these points out can help reassure each other that you plan to be fair and mindful of the impact with this life change.

Let go of the idea that there's such a thing as breaking up "smoothly." We often think that as long as we can say just the right thing, the conversation will go well. But relationships are not business transactions. It'll be easier if you're realistic about what to expect. It will almost always be an emotionally intense conversation.

Be kind and honest. Remember:

- No matter how it may seem, you are both resilient and will both make it through this.

- Change is hard, but people can adapt.

- Treat your partner the way you want to be treated.

- Both of you will gain different perspectives over time, and healing will be easier if you do the best you can to be fair now.

- The emotional intensity of this time will not last forever.

- People are more resilient than they realize.

- Endings help us assess what kind of life we want to live.

Will I regret leaving?

I sometimes wish this question would be more realistic. People cycle through many emotions; it's part of being human. Regret is just one of those emotions. And, like all emotions (good and bad), it is temporary.

How you feel will depend on where you are in the recovery process, but regret tends to fade as you rebuild. And a new, healthy love relationship can help with healing. My personal thought is that once you are in a place where you're getting your needs met (no matter your relationship status), contentment pushes regret to the back burner.

Difficulties help us learn about ourselves and the kind of lives we need to be content. I believe this is why research shows that people tend to get wiser and happier as they get older. The more we know about ourselves, the more we can build a life with happiness and meaning.

Most of the people who weighed in here wished they had realized sooner that things weren't working, perhaps because couples do not seek help until they have been unhappy for an average of six years. (Gaspard, MSW, LICSW. Timing is Everything. 2015. https:// www.gottman.com/blog/timing-is-everything-when-it-comes-to-marriage-counseling) Happily, many people find love and happiness again, and most people remain hopeful about the future.

Chapter 11

What do I do now? I'm all alone.

This is cliché, but the best thing to do is to bite off small pieces you can chew. The first one is to set your expectations. It may sound simplistic, but it can actually help to anticipate feeling crummy.

When the weather forecast predicts a storm, we prepare. We stock up on non-perishables and flashlights and generally set our expectations to match the situation. You wouldn't plan an outdoor barbeque. The same outlook can help ease an oncoming rough time.

Most of the people who answered this survey said that they realized only later that they had expectations that weren't realistic. They underestimated how much time they needed to process the breakup, how hard it might be to be alone, how long it might take to get into a new routine, and even how much energy they'd have on any given day.

Set your expectations very low. On some days, just breathing will be enough.

Important points:

- Become comfortable with being uncomfortable: it will likely be the norm for longer than you'd like.

- Be kind to yourself: compassion and self-care are the antidotes for anguish.

- No one finds themselves at the end of a relationship feeling like everything went splendidly. Do not beat yourself up over mistakes. It will not accelerate the healing process. There will be time for inner reflection and growth, but that's only possible when you can face yourselves with grace and compassion.

- Be your own BFF, too; imagine the advice you would give to them, and that will help guide you.

- People who are hurting tend to hurt other people. Try to remember that pain makes it very difficult for people to show up as their best selves. It's best not to internalize unkind behavior.

Coping skills

It's hard to go through a breakup alone. Assemble a network of support: start counseling, reach out to friends, and search for online forums, apps, groups, or organizations to connect with a community. Visit a bookstore and spend some time in the self-help section. Write yourself letters from your older, wiser self. Read memoirs. Listen to comedy channels. Watch movies. Take baths. Blast the radio. Dance. Cook. Write.

---

8 things you can do to make your life more emotionally stable
by Dr. Nicole LePera

Emotional stability is key in feeling content and fulfilled.

1. **Don't make assumptions:** if you're wondering why someone did something or why they didn't do something, ask. We all create stories in our minds about people's intentions that are rarely true. Communication is key.

2. **Speak your needs and expectations:** so many of us expect people to be mind readers. No one can understand what we need unless we openly tell them.

3. **Get comfortable with saying no:** say no regularly to things that drain your energy, make you feel uninspired, or that takes you away from what you're prioritizing. All fulfilled people have clear boundaries.

---

4. **Find some way to give back:** this can mean giving time, energy, offering your skill set, or financial support. Giving back and serving something bigger than your self helps to create that community connection. This sense of belonging is healing.

5. **Dedicate time each week to doing something you love**, just for you. It's important to have unstructured time for play, creativity, exploration without needing any specific end result.

6. **Learn how to regulate your emotions.** This means learning how to feel and accept emotions, rather than habitually reacting to your emotions. This gives you greater control over your responses and your overall behavior.

7. **Spend time in nature.** Nature is the greatest healer. Get in the sun, be among the trees, discover a new trial. This is a complete reset for the nervous system.

8. **Unsubscribe from urgency culture.** Put space between automatically answering texts, emails, or other people's crisis. Check in with yourself first–are you in a place to respond? If not, respond when you are.

SOURCE: @theholisticpsyc on Twitter:
https://twitter.com/theholisticpsyc/status/1580952719442862080

What about the legal process?

Be kind and fair. Ten years from now, you will want to be able to live with the decisions you are making now, and you don't want to feel like you've ruined someone, acted unfairly, or allowed yourself to be treated unfairly.

An advice columnist once said, "Do the right thing. Add in your feelings and 'the right thing' may hurt like hell, but hasn't changed."

You'll know the right thing to do. Be motivated by that and not by feelings.

Feelings of anger, guilt, remorse, sadness, grief—those are all normal and hurt incredibly intensely but should not influence your path. Your journey will involve making peace with your past, and you won't be able to do this if driven by negativity.

Tips:

- **Consider an initial consultation with a lawyer** to find out more about what separating might look like for your situation. These are usually free.

- **Would a mediator work?** Consider mediation if things are amicable and uncomplicated. It can be much less costly, but this approach won't work for everyone. If you're not sure, it's worth an initial consult with a mediator and attorney (or two or three) to explore.

- **Research** whoever you consider hiring thoroughly. You need someone who will look out for your best interests and also be ethical and fair. Part of this research may involve meeting with the professional you're considering for a consultation, so you know whether the rapport and expertise are there. An additional benefit to this is that you may find several attorneys saying the same things about likely outcomes and giving the same advice. This will bolster confidence in your options and may enable you to do it yourself.

- **If you're contemplating doing it yourself,** scrutinize your situation carefully. The best predictor for how things may unfold in the aftermath is how conflict went before. If your partner exhibited toxic behaviors while you were together, expect this to continue, especially when emotions are raw.

- **Keep in mind:** Communication can be tricky when going through a third party or email; text is very dry and lacks tone and context. Remembering this can help offset frustration.

Chapter 12

How can I move forward?

You can't move past bad feelings unless you let yourself feel them, so feel them. Process with a counselor and mourn, grieve, rage, question … whatever comes up, give it room. Let the emotions come out however feels best. Write, walk, move, talk, create, dance, paint, sing, put on a mud-mask … anything goes.

Write yourself love letters from future you who can look back and know you made it. Browse advice columns and anonymous forums. Read poetry. Explore libraries and bookstores. Cook. Bird-watch. Find podcasts. Play comedy on loops. Take a class.

The best way forward is to just be and breathe.

The heart will heal in time, and this will pass.

It's like that old saying: "this too shall pass" … it may pass like a kidney stone, but it *will* pass!

With time and new experiences, perspective can shift. And this can be very powerful.

User *Softly_stepping* on Reddit wrote:

> *It felt like my world had ended, everything was wrecked, and nothing could ever possibly be good again. I had a complete mental breakdown. I couldn't eat or sleep. I'd break into fits of uncontrollable crying multiple times each day. I thought I was losing my mind. I started contemplating suicide as a way to escape from the pain.*
>
> *Other people I'd spoken to encouraged me in my grief and rage. "Oh, you poor thing, you must be devastated!" "No wonder you're so angry; your husband's such an asshole!" I took a lot of pleasure in crying and venting, but at the end of the day I still felt upset and out of control. Why was this happening to me? Why couldn't I do anything about it? It was*

so fucking unfair! Why was he treating me this way? Why had I married such a dickhead? My life was wasted; my life was over.

But my therapist refused to indulge my wild emotions. Instead, she encouraged me to calm myself, to stop blaming myself and my husband, to stop seeing myself as a victim and divorce as evidence that my life was wasted or that I was a failure. She understood that I felt destroyed by this crisis. And, yes, it had been destructive. I gazed at my life and saw only ruin, but she suggested that there was another way to look at things.

I could choose to remain sunk in misery and self-pity. Or I could choose to see this crisis as an opportunity for growth and change, a chance to shake myself out of the patterns that had been limiting me.

She described the pieces of my life as fitting together like tiles on a game board. There was comfort in that stability, but it was also stifling: the pattern was set and locked, and I couldn't move for fear of upsetting everything.

And then, she told me, the crisis happens, the board is flipped, and the pieces all fly up in the air. It feels like everything is over. When the pieces come back down, the familiar pattern will be gone. It's left to you to pick them up and put them back together, and that feels so difficult and unfair.

And yet, the situation that has brought such pain and hardship also presents you with an opportunity, a chance to do something different. You can examine and judge each piece in turn, throw away the ones you don't want any more and replace them with new ones. You can lay them back down in a new pattern, one that suits you better. You can listen to your heart and do what you want, free from constraint.

You must change, for you have no choice, but you have the power to direct that change. I found this metaphor to be incredibly inspiring. Once I really internalized it, it completely changed the way I viewed my situation. Divorce wasn't something I'd asked for. It wasn't something I'd wanted. But it was something that had happened and I could choose to deal with it in a positive manner or a negative one.

And that was something else she told me: I cannot control this situation. I cannot control my husband. But I can control how I react. That is, in fact, the only thing I truly can control. And it is not a stretch to say that embracing this mindset has changed my life.

Five months ago I was miserable, feeling trapped in an unhappy marriage. Four months ago I was an absolute wreck, feeling like my life was over. Today, I'm feeling confident and proud, and I'm looking forward to each new day. I never wanted a divorce, but it has been a chance to improve myself and my life - a chance that, honestly, I never thought I'd have. I'm determined not to waste it.

I don't know if this will help anyone else, but it feels like a thing worth writing, in case it might bring someone else here some comfort in the midst of grief and pain. Things can get better. You have the power to make it so.

SOURCE: https://www.reddit.com/r/Divorce/comments/r8n67y/seeing_opportunity_in_crisis_my_therapists/

Take the time you need.

What about the kids?

There's no way around this—the impact on kids can be substantial. Almost everyone who answered my survey wished they had brought in extra support for their kids right away. Many delayed breaking up in order to protect them.

There are so many factors that affect well-being: make sure kids know they are loved and have access to counseling, support, and privacy so they can work through their feelings.

Some tips:

- Do not send messages to each other through the kids. They should not be responsible for planning, scheduling, or communicating information that parents need to relay to each other.

- Be conscious of how you speak about the other parent around your kids. Negativity, even when it seems justified, still does not serve the kids' best interests. Kids only get one set of parents, and a divorce is hard enough without putting additional burdens on them to divide loyalty.

- Don't share marital issues with kids.

- Do not let anyone else discipline your kids. This includes new partners. Of course, you cannot control how your soon-to-be-ex behaves. But on your watch, only parents should parent.

- Try to keep things as stable as possible for them.

- Be mindful about sharing concerns about things that may affect their sense of security, such as money or whether or not food will be available. It's okay to share that there's a new budget or that there are new limitations; this sets an example of how to adjust to life circumstances, a useful lifelong skill.

- You don't have to figure everything out. If something feels large and overwhelming to manage, it's probably because it is and you need help managing it. You don't have to handle things all alone. Reach out to family, community, or professionals for assistance.

- Try to give kids the message that you are all resilient and will get through this. It's okay to be yourself—you don't have to hide how you're feeling. But if you're struggling, it's good to set an example of self-care and get counseling help if possible so you can lean on a support network.

- Let kids feel how they feel. Give them as much support as you can, including counseling with a therapist they trust and feel comfortable with, if possible. Keep the lines of communication open and your connection strong.

- It's okay if kids aren't happy all the time. It would be impossible to do anyway. As long as you prioritize and love them, you're doing great.

If you navigate with help and care, kids will eventually learn resilience, a skill that will serve them for the rest of their lives. Studies show resilience—or grit—is more tied to success than intelligence (Berger, Michele. "What Factors Predict Success?" Penn Today. 2019. https://penntoday.upenn.edu/news/Penn-Angela-Duckworth-looks-beyond-grit-predict-success).

How long does it take to get over a breakup?

Healing from a breakup takes more time than we'd like. And even if we *know* this, being in the thick of it can still take your breath away. The five stages of grief apply to loss, not just death. Divorce is not just a breakup—it's also the loss of the hopes and dreams you once built.

> *"We can't fully experience and share in one another's losses. No one else is living your grief or has had your loss.... Your relationship was unique, and so your loss is unique. What you miss about them, what you wish you had or hadn't said, the memories you made or could have made together—these belong only to you."*
>
> ~Janine Kwoh, *Welcome to the Grief Club*

Recovery times vary and depend on many factors: if and how much disconnection was occurring in the relationship, which side of the ending you're on, whether there are any complicated co-occuring conditions like depression or rejection-sensitive dysphoria, what kind of support network you can assemble, how confident you feel in being able to direct the course of your life, and more. Often the biggest predictor of recovery is however long it takes you to find a new, healthy love relationship.

But don't rush into a new relationship while things are terribly raw and you're not ready to be fully present for a new partner. There is some thought that a new relationship can help the heart heal, but it's not a linear process. We cannot flip a switch, but over time, tendrils from the past recede and roots from the present begin to grow.

Transitions generally take two to three years, but it's best not to have a timeline in mind. That way you can let yourself feel how you feel without shaming yourself for not "getting over it" more quickly.

Blended families tend to take even longer, as they cycle through stages: as little as 4 or as many as 12 years (but average time frame is 9 years). (Papernow, Patricia, Ed.D. *Patterns of Development in Stepfamilies.* 1999. https://www.steptogether.org/development.html)

What do I do with the almost paralyzing shame of things not working out?

People hesitate to take steps because the costs of disruption are so high. And society stigmatizes struggle, shaming people for the perception of "failure" (not just with relationships but with jobs, homes, parenting, health, schooling). Anything that doesn't seem to "work out" as planned is game for shame. Somehow we are supposed to have figured it all out despite having no control over other people or even the final outcome.

There is no rulebook that says things have to happen a certain way and that we aren't allowed to make mistakes or shift course as we learn. We do not need to stick with situations that no longer work or punish ourselves for not having the right resources or understanding. No one is expected to fly through the air with superhero relationship capes, relating perfectly to everyone around us all the time. We are mortal. Being human is complicated.

Do you know what helps? Having compassion. People all face different trials. The best antidote for shame is connection. Seek a support network where you can safely open up. Ask your counselor or check out the following anonymous forums:

- **r/KindVoice:** https://www.reddit.com/r/KindVoice/

- **r/Divorce:** https://www.reddit.com/r/Divorce/

- **r/Relationships:** https://www.reddit.com/r/relationships/

- **r/MomForAMinute:** https://www.reddit.com/r/MomForAMinute/

- **r/DadForAMinute:** https://www.reddit.com/r/DadForAMinute/

- **r/ToastMe:** https://www.reddit.com/r/toastme/

There are groups for nearly every topic. You can search using any keyword on Reddit or on search engines, or you can ask your counselor, or call 211 for resources.

Always be careful and mindful about internet safety, privacy, and security.

How do I say I'm sorry?

You may find yourself wishing for a way to express deep sorrow. People usually feel sorrow for what they are going through in addition to the pain their partners, kids, families, pets, and even extended communities experience. It can be healing to acknowledge this, whether it comes in the form of an honest conversation, an apology, or an internal monologue.

Apologizing doesn't have to mean admitting fault or taking blame. It also doesn't mean singularly accepting wrongdoing. It is just part of feeling and expressing sorrow.

Heartfelt remorse acknowledges impact and can go a long way to healing and mending bridges.

However, if hoping for closure, be mindful of people's boundaries. If someone does not want to engage, respect their feelings and do not violate their wishes. You can still move forward by forgiving yourself and vowing to grow from the experience. Self-compassion is the biggest part of healing. Time can bring gifts of understanding and peace.

How can I stay connected with mutual friends and family after the divorce?

Not everyone will be comfortable maintaining a relationship with both partners after they split. Try not to speak poorly of your ex, and don't make the mistake of asking anyone to take sides. Also, be selective when confiding your side of the story; don't share intimate, personal details with people who are not in your specific inner circle. It can be tempting to open up when asked because the yearning to be understood is so powerful, but that can put mutual friends in an awkward place.

If you do share, refer to your history with as much kindness and fairness as possible. The ex has a side, too, and they are not in the room to defend themselves, so it isn't quite fair to complain about them. You can be honest about the things that were hard and still be kind by acknowledging that your ex also struggled; pain is not under limited copyright and ownership.

Even those with a more visible role in the relationship's demise may be in pain too. Try to remember that you both once cared for each other, and draw from that well of respect when chatting with mutual acquaintances. Even if it seems like your ex could have managed things better, not everyone is able to face things with high levels of self-awareness and accountability. It depends on their emotional health and comfort with introspection and vulnerability. Your ex may not be there (yet or ever), but you won't need to explain their defense mechanisms to others; they may already realize what goes unsaid. Healing will be a little easier if you focus on the gains rather than the losses.

Chapter 13

Rebuilding

Any advice for reentering the dating world? What tips might make it less awkward and painful?

Know what you need.

If you know that you need a certain amount of connectedness in a relationship, then you're not going to be satisfied with not getting it. Likewise, if you know you need a certain amount of space, you won't be happy not having that.

You must know what you need.

It is so crucial to know this (and turn away the wrong people) that it's worth keeping two lists: one of non-negotiables and another of nice-to-haves. For example, if you know you want children someday, and learn over coffee that your new date is profoundly against having a family, then it's not wise to dive in hoping they may change their mind. It's always better to make decisions based on the reality that exists now.

Many people become attached to those they are physical with. Our biology influences this by secreting oxytocin and other bonding hormones. Being selective can help the brain stay in charge while still getting to know each other.

For great information on the science of dating, see Dr. Duana Welch's *"Love Factually"* series for singles and single parents, or her short ebook topics on a variety of relationship subjects. She covers the biological reasons why men and women act the way they do when dating and why certain strategies are more successful than others.

How do I pick a good partner?

After a major breakup, we often feel vulnerable about the idea of loving again. How do we make sure to pick someone who's a good match?

One good way to tell is to observe your feelings. Do you feel at ease with them? Or do you feel like you're trying to prove yourself somehow or "get" them to like you? If so, consider how exhausting that would be long-term.

If you notice you're drawn to people who make you feel inadequate or unvalued, that can be a sign of revisiting unhealthy patterns from your formative years. We tend to be drawn to people who feel familiar, but if "familiar" wasn't healthy, this can lead to recreating self-destructive dynamics.

Politely and kindly move on if you realize there's a mismatch, but don't ask anyone to explain themselves or overly express your own feelings. If interactions leave you feeling bad about yourself, that's a sign to let it go. Move toward people and activities that fulfill you, not make you question whether your needs or wants are valid.

A fulfilling relationship is not tied to whether all the boxes are checked on your want list. It's tied to the way you both interact and connect.

> *"Dr. John Gottman, the founder of The Gottman Institute in Seattle, said that measures of personality are incapable of truly predicting the length or success of a relationship. Gottman discovered that couples who focus their energy on building something meaningful together in their life (e.g., starting a business together) tend to last the longest. How a couple interacts is the single, most fundamental aspect to creating a successful relationship. Meaning, it's not who you are or what you do that will prolong or help you find the perfect mate. It's how you speak to each other, how well you get along, and how you move through time together."*
>
> ~ L.R. Borbón
>
> (From: https://www.gottman.com/blog/psychology-finally-reveals-the-answer-to-finding-your-soulmate)

Dating can be exhausting. How do I manage my energy?

There are four possibilities for every person you meet:

1. You both like each other.
2. They like you, but you don't like them.
3. You like them, but they don't like you.
4. Neither of you like each other.

It takes time to see which outcome will surface because people get to know each other incrementally, so it tends to take about three to five months on average. The most tiring part is usually the loss of hope when it doesn't work out and you have to start over.

But if you were home-hunting, you'd scope out lots of places.

You would ask, "Do I want this home?"

Not "Does this place want me?"

Try to keep perspective.

If you stay grounded, you'll be able to keep meeting new folks without getting so weary that you just give up when you really want companionship. It's okay to take breaks as needed.

It also helps to not to take mismatches personally.

Reasons have nothing to do with your worthiness. We don't usually feel hurt if someone gets hungry or thirsty more often than we do, but for some reason, clashes on emotional needs can sting. It's important to stay rooted.

You are worthy of love. If you loved deeply before, that is proof you are capable of love, which is the one main ingredient for finding it again.

Exercise:

Write a letter from your future self to your current self. Your future self understands this time from a much greater perspective and can be there for you now.

For example:

> Dear self,
>
> You are a beautiful and worthy human being. You are sweet and kind and genuinely care about people. Yes, you are hurting now, but you should know that one person's reaction to you doesn't define you. If there is anything that is your fault in that painful scenario, it is in believing that someone else's frailties signify your worthiness. Your own frailty is in hoping that love alone is enough.
>
> This is a painful process, this putting one foot in front of the other and moving forward. You don't know where it will land. You've successfully embodied the teachings of Buddhists who say "live in the moment!" to the point where it's hard to imagine a future in which you will be in love again and feel loved back. I know it feels like that will never happen, but you are doing the hard work now that points to being in a stronger place later (the Magic 8 Ball says "all signs point to yes!").
>
> Some days all you can do is breathe.
>
> So, breathe.
>
> When you are in a place where you can climb again, you will ... put one foot in front of the other and attempt to ascend this mountain.

You are now building a life for yourself
where you get to call the shots; you get
to decide what you want it to look like.
In the past, it was defined by others. Now
it's defined by you. That's scary—you don't
know how. Having never quite done just this,
you're unsure of your footing, but that's OK.
You will make mistakes and learn from them.
Like a baby learning to walk, you will fall
down and get up and try again and again. It's
not the falling down that matters but the
getting back up.

So fall, often.

Love, as much as possible. If the love isn't
returned, well, you loved regardless of it
being returned, right? You gave it because
you could not help it, you felt that way and
it was a beautiful gift, it shows that you
are a person capable of deep caring. Don't be
scared to do this over and over again; one
of the most beautiful gifts we can give in
life is to truly care about another person.
That doesn't make you bad. Yes, it hurts, but
that you were able to experience that kind of
depth alone is worthy of recognition. One day
your efforts will be returned to you and you
will be surrounded by the kind of love you
can freely give. It's hard to picture now—you
don't know what that will look like, but it
will be there. Because if you can give love
like that, some of it is bound to return.

love,
me

Hang in there, friend.

Why do second and subsequent marriages have a higher breakup rate?

It's challenging to bring complicated lives together when people have built previous families, careers, and lifestyles. There's more history and less flexibility in the structures of our lives and in ourselves.

I also think it's possible that people are less apprehensive of the process the next time around because they've been there before. They survived and "rebuilt." They now know the power of their own resilience. They also recognize issues more quickly and may not want to invest further when feeling constraints of time or other resources.

> *"Resilience isn't staying steadfast on a path that no longer exists. Resilience is doing the messy, hard, and slow work of creating a new life when the old one is no longer an option."*
> ~Janine Kwoh, *Welcome to the Grief Club*

How can I do better next time around? I don't want to get divorced again.

Obviously, no one gets married thinking it won't work out. But we don't have complete control over how things will go in our lives. Indeed, this is the single most difficult concept to relinquish throughout our lives: the idea that we can secure a particular outcome.

However, we now understand so much more about what helps relationships succeed and what can make even the most fervent love fail, thanks to extensive research.

I became interested in this topic after my divorce and went on to become a trained Gottman Educator from the Gottman Institute, renowned for their decades of studies on relationships.

I'll do my best to summarize some of their work here, but a good place to start is with the book *The Seven Principles for Making Marriage Work* by Dr. John Gottman, or check out their extensive resources online (including videos, podcasts, articles, apps, and more): https://www.gottman.com.

There appear to be two main factors that play crucial roles in couples' happiness: **friendship** and **safety**.

Of course, many other factors play roles too, such as compatibility, conflict resolution, communication, personality, history, and more, but the most important ones distill down to how safe people feel together (unconsciously), and whether they are good friends to each other.

This is very vague, however. What does it mean to feel safe? To be good friends? Let's explore it.

What is friendship? What does it mean to be a good friend?

- A good friend feels like a person who is there for you (they "have your back").

- They won't criticize you, make fun of you, or betray your trust.

- They give you the benefit of the doubt if there's a misunderstanding; they assume you are trying your best and are not out to hurt them or sabotage the relationship.

- They prioritize kindness and generosity. (See https://www.theatlantic.com/health/archive/2014/06/happily-ever-after/372573/)

- They reciprocate and help maintain a healthy balance of give and take that feels equal.

- They ensure both partners' needs and feelings are prioritized.

- They are tuned in enough to realize if you're not able to listen, be present, or otherwise reciprocate the way they wish, and they accept this.

- They don't regularly ask or expect things that hurt the other person. For example, they understand when you need sleep even if they would prefer for you to stay up with them. A good friend accepts limitations and boundaries without internalizing another's needs maliciously.

- You feel valued and appreciated with them.

Now how about safety—how does safety show up in our relationships? What makes a person feel safe?

What is safety?

- You can be yourself.

- You can trust that your partner is invested in your relationship and not on the verge of leaving.

- You can share what you think and feel without worrying about their reaction. (The ability to manage strong feelings helps partners feel safe. The Gottmans found that how conflict begins determines how the rest of it will go—if it can begin on a calm note, chances are much better for discussion and understanding.)

- Most of the time, when you reach out for your partner, even in small ways, they respond positively. (The Gottmans call this "bids for connection" because they are opportunities to connect. Research found that happy couples turned toward each other around 86% of the time, but at-risk couples only turned toward each other 33% of the time. https://www. gottman.com/blog/turn-toward-instead-of-away)

However, studies found that couples at risk showed signs of being in fight-or-flight mode around each other. They didn't even need to realize this—researchers could measure elevated heart rates, skin perspiration, and the presence of stress hormones, all signs of alarm bells from the autonomic nervous system, whether or not they were aware. There was something about the presence or interaction that made their bodies react as if they were unsafe.

Why?

Well, the brain is a wet, squishy, pattern-detection computer that constantly scans the environment to assess your safety. It examines everything you experience and runs it through a database in order to assign meaning.

The last time your partner yelled, did their eye twitch?

Well, the next time the brain sees an eye twitch—even from a completely different eye—it may predict doom, triggering your fight-or-flight response.

This is to keep you safe, so you have enough energy to either flee from the tiger or fight off the wolf.

Unfortunately, the human stress response has not changed much since early times, so everything that is catalogued as a threat is met with one of four strategies:

- Fight
- Flight
- Freeze
- Fawn

The threat doesn't need to be physical in order to catch your brain's attention. Emotional "threats" will also trigger the stress response, and that's what research found. Somehow the couples at risk were in a state of elevated stress around each other.

Trauma, abuse, and conflict histories complicate how safe people feel and should be professionally treated. A threat doesn't need to fit a certain definition or appear a certain way in order to trigger someone. All it needs is for the individual's brain to have catalogued it as a threat at some point in their lives. Mannerisms, smells, textures, lighting, or even the seemingly simple quest of being close or just being vulnerable can be triggers.

The science does not specifically point out *what* was triggering to the at-risk folks, only that they *were* triggered around each other. They didn't always know it, but their bodies did.

Studies also found that for every negative interaction, *five* positive interactions were needed just to cancel it out to bring it to zero.

It's not a 1:1 ratio where one fight can be smoothed over by one makeup hug; five positives for every one negative just brings it back to neutral ground. In order to tip the scales to happiness, 20 positives are needed for every one negative. (Benson, Kyle. *The Magic Relationship Ratio, According to Science.* The Gottman Institute Blog. 2023. https://www.gottman.com/blog/the-magic-relationship-ratio-according-science)

How to build safety

What's the most central component to building safety?

This may seem loosely connected, but it's actually key: self-care.

This is because self-care involves being in touch with your needs, and being in touch with your needs means that feelings, our internal messengers, do not need to shout to get your attention.

If you notice when you're hungry, tired, emotionally taxed, or any of the myriad things a human experiences in a given day, you can do something about these things. Feelings arise from unmet needs.

What happens when people feel angry, frustrated, lonely, unheard, disconnected, or any type of negative feeling? It would be a rare wizard who never reacted but learning to keep the reaction in check can help those around feel safe. When people begin to lose their tempers, it not only means they are in fight-or-flight mode, but so are those around them, whether or not they're in the direct path.

Learning to react differently (if you want to) is possible, but it can take a while. However, you can see an immediate reduction in negative feelings if you plug into your needs.

So, **the best relationship care is actually self-care.**

Marshall Rosenberg, founder of the Center for Nonviolent Communication, talks about the importance of knowing ourselves and thus knowing what we need:

> *What I often encounter in my work, is that people try to have different feelings than they do. They say "I want to feel happy" or "I want to feel comfortable with my body" or "I don't want to be scared anymore." It's often hard to give up on the aim to have or don't have a certain feeling.*
>
> *Feelings are never stable. Our feelings change every few seconds. We can't control what's going to happen next and which feelings will result from whatever happens. To have this goal of having a certain feeling is not a very achievable goal.*
>
> *Instead I recommend this way of viewing feelings: the feeling is never the problem. The problem isn't that you're scared or uncomfortable or unhappy. That's not the problem. The problem is that your needs aren't met. It's good that you have those feelings, but you need to make sure to not stop at the feeling, but connect to what your need is that creates the feeling. Imagine a world where you can't feel the feeling of hunger. You'd never know when the body needs food. You'd starve and not even know it.*
>
> *It's good that you have those uncomfortable feelings. They tell you that your needs aren't met. The problem is that in our culture, you're not at all trained to connect your feelings with needs. Most of us don't know what we need. So what we're trying to do is to change our feelings. That can only work short term. Instead, look for your need and find a way to meet your need. That's what will make a difference.*

Sometimes couples disconnect from each other because it's the best way they know of to take care of themselves. Surprisingly, disconnection was found to be the top risk for separation, not conflict. (However, conflict can lead to disconnection as people withdraw in fight, flight, or freeze mode.)

The key to managing conflict is not to avoid it. Conflict itself isn't bad—it's how it's handled and received that makes the difference between high-risk and low-risk couples.

Research studies found that 69% of problems in a relationship are not solvable. However, issues do not need to be fixed in order for a couple to be happy. They just need to feel understood.

Feeling understood moves problems from working memory to storage memory so the brain no longer needs to continue processing. I call this "closing the tab"—your computer doesn't need to keep that browser tab open, running resources to maintain it in the background.

You can find techniques for making each other feel understood and for handling "gridlock" (when problems seem stuck) in Dr. Gottman's book, *The Seven Principles for Making Marriage Work* (mentioned earlier), or Google "Gridlock Gottman" to find examples.

Also central to connection is finding time to talk—not just chatter about household logistics, but about deeper things, like how the day went and how each other are feeling.

Research found that carving out **20 minutes a day** to connect helped couples feel more bonded. It may seem hard to believe, but many couples did not have even this scant amount of time free. Life's demands rarely cease. Try to make time together a priority.

Dr. Gottman's research has also identified four key behaviors that negatively affect relationship satisfaction. Because their presence predicted divorce with 93% accuracy, Gottman designated them "the Four Horsemen" (named after the reference to the biblical Four Horsemen of the Apocalypse). These behaviors, described below, are toxic and undermine connection:

The Four Horsemen:

1. **Criticism** hinders the desired outcome: to solve a problem. It also wears many hats: poking fun, questioning, belittling, shaming, or anything that shifts the power balance from equal peers to one where judgment is bestowed is criticism. Criticism makes people feel bad. Reword criticism to a complaint instead, emphasizing your feelings and the impact on you, and what you need instead.

   Don't say: "You're such a slob!"
   Do say: "I have trouble concentrating when the house is messy. Can you put laundry in your hamper instead of on the floor?"

2. **Contempt** communicates disgust and is particularly dangerous, especially over time. It usually has the effect of making someone feel devalued. Contempt can also be conveyed nonverbally, such as with eye-rolling and frustrated sighs.

   Don't say: "He cannot cook to save his life!"
   Do say: "He doesn't enjoy cooking as much as I do, but we both like to eat out!"

3. **Defensiveness** usually involves deflecting and does not help the couple move toward understanding or a resolution.

   An example of defensiveness is responding to a complaint with a complaint. Usually when people defend themselves, it's because they feel attacked. Sometimes rephrasing can help soften the delivery.

   Partner A:

   "I'd really like some help cleaning up after dinner."

Partner B:

Don't say: "But you left the last mess all to me!"
Do say: "Okay, how can I help?"

4. **Stonewalling** is when people shut down and stop communicating. Problems can't be resolved if they're not aired. However, people need to feel safe in order to open up. A big reason people go silent is because they are flooded and have entered fight-or-flight mode.

Flooding

If your heart rate is 20 beats per minute more than usual, that is a sign that of being in fight-or-flight mode and the thinking region of the brain has shut down. This is known as "flooding."

Flooding is a physiological response and leads people to be unable to take in any more information so further dialogue is not helpful. The senses are overwhelmed and at capacity.

It takes *at least* 17 minutes for stress hormones to leave the body when triggered so the best way to manage this is to take a short break.

Agree to revisit the topic afterwards, and then try not to think about it while cooling off (otherwise that will keep the system flooded with stress hormones). Try to revisit it within a reasonable time frame. Longer than 24 hours is generally too long and can be felt as punishment. Ideally, wait 20–30 minutes.

While the "Four Horsemen" behaviors are harmful in love relationships, these principles apply to all relationships. Family, friends, colleagues, neighbors, acquaintances, and more. Good communication is the foundation for healthy relationships.

Communication can also be complicated by factors out of our full control, like stress, medical conditions, history, trauma, mood disorders, neurological differences in wiring and even communication style. Many things influence the ways we relate to each other and how we show up in the world, and they vary constantly. Therapy can help with skills for coping with stress, communicating, and understanding the unmet needs that underlie turmoil.

Conflict itself isn't necessarily an issue; on the other side of every dispute is the opportunity for greater understanding. If a couple can mend their bond, they can become closer. How conflict starts tends to determine the rest of the conversation so approaching issues respectfully is key. Soften the startup and be mindful of the negative behaviors of the Four Horsemen to connect more deeply and resolve differences.

Nonviolent Communication or NVC (also known as Compassionate Communication) is a powerful technique for learning to listen and talk without using language in ways that shut people down. It's also a good tool for self-regulation as it teaches how to identify what we need.

Unmet needs are at the core of almost all conflict and tension, including internal tension. The single most valuable ingredient for contentment is recognizing how we feel and what we need and NVC's focus on connection makes it a worthy practice. (*The Center for Nonviolent Communication*[SM] https://www.cnvc.org)

We may never have wanted to join the Breakup Club but if we remember that our experiences add to us, we can take what we've learned and begin building better tomorrows out of our todays.

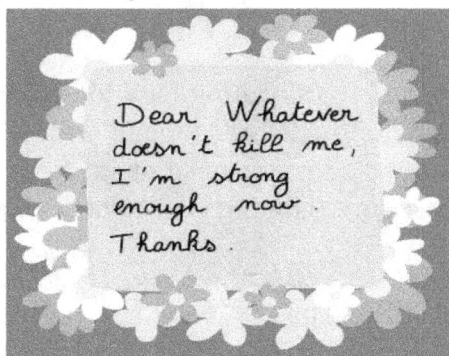

Anne-Claire Regan - @hiboudesigns

4 Myths About Relationships

From Esther Perel

Myth 1: We Should Be able to Tell Our Partners Everything.

Some people believe that intimacy means knowing everything about each other. But one person can't be our confidant for all. Certain things are better shared with friends, therapists, and siblings.

Myth 2: If you knew me, you would know…

There's a notion that our partners should know us so well that we shouldn't have to say what we are needing or feeling. But we have to be able to speak to what we want; our partners are not extensions of ourselves.

Myth 3: Our Partners Can Be Everything Our Parents Were Not

Our partners can give us a lot. They can fill us with the love we have been deprived of and offer us trust and safety like we've never known. But they don't owe us to make up for the deprivations of our childhood. It is their gift, not their responsibility.

Myth 4: If They Change, Things Will Get Better

That thinking can keep us waiting for a long time. And absolutes are sure to backfire, leaving us with defensiveness on both sides. Loosen the knot: instead of attempting to change your partner, focus on changing your relationship. That takes both of you.

SOURCE: https://www.instagram.com/p/CUsz4pCLmUw/

. . .
Poems
. . .

my brain and heart divorced

by John Roedel

my brain and
heart divorced

a decade ago

over who was
to blame about
how big of a mess
I have become

eventually,
they couldn't be
in the same room
with each other

now my head and heart
share custody of me

I stay with my brain
during the week

and my heart
gets me on weekends

they never speak to one another
  - instead, they give me
the same note to pass
to each other every week

and their notes they
send to one another always
says the same thing:

"This is all your fault"

on Sundays
my heart complains

about how my
head has let me down
in the past

and on Wednesday
my head lists all
of the times my
heart has screwed
things up for me
in the future

they blame each
other for the
state of my life

there's been a lot
of yelling - and crying

so,

   lately, I've been
spending a lot of
time with my gut

who serves as my
unofficial therapist

most nights, I sneak out of the
window in my ribcage

and slide down my spine
and collapse on my
gut's plush leather chair
that's always open for me

~ and I just sit sit sit sit
until the sun comes up

last evening,
my gut asked me

if I was having a hard
time being caught
between my heart
and my head

I nodded

I said I didn't know
if I could live with
either of them anymore

"my heart is always sad about
something that happened yesterday
while my head is always worried
about something that may happen tomorrow,"

I lamented

my gut squeezed my hand

"I just can't live with
my mistakes of the past
or my anxiety about the future,"
I sighed

my gut smiled and said:

"in that case,
you should
go stay with your
lungs for a while,"

I was confused
 - the look on my face gave it away

"if you are exhausted about
your heart's obsession with
the fixed past and your mind's focus
on the uncertain future

your lungs are the perfect place for you

there is no yesterday in your lungs
there is no tomorrow there either

there is only now
there is only inhale
there is only exhale
there is only this moment

there is only breath

and in that breath
you can rest while your
heart and head work
their relationship out."

this morning,
while my brain
was busy reading
tea leaves

and while my
heart was staring
at old photographs

I packed a little
bag and walked
to the door of
my lungs

before I could even knock
she opened the door
with a smile and as
a gust of air embraced me
she said

"what took you so long?"

www.johnroedel.com

The Cure

by Albert Huffstickler

We think we get over things.
We don't get over things.
Or say, we get over the measles
but not a broken heart.
We need to make that distinction.
The things that become part of our experience
never become less a part of our experience.
How can I say it?
The way to "get over" a life is to die.
Short of that, you move with it,
let the pain be pain,
not in the hope that it will vanish
but in the faith that it will fit in,
find its place in the shape of things
and be then not any less pain but true to form.
Because anything natural has an inherent shape
and will flow towards it.
And a life is as natural as a leaf.
That's what we're looking for:
not the end of a thing but the shape of it.
Wisdom is seeing the shape of your life
without obliterating (getting over) a single
instant of it.

Untitled

by John Roedel

this isn't how I planned for
my life to look like," I whispered
under my breath as I walked to my car

"tell me about it,"
an eavesdropping cloud
replied to me from above

I looked up and watched
the cloud billow between looking
like a dove and an open hand

the cloud continued:

"I used to be a snowfield in Montana.
I used to be a dewdrop kiss on a lily.
I used to be a puddle in a parking lot.
I used to be a river in Mexico.
I used to be a glacier.
I used to be a waterfall mist in a jungle.

I used to be so many things."

"doesn't that make you sad?" I asked the cloud

"it used to—but not anymore," the cloud replied while wrapping herself around
me like a scarf. "I don't think either of us were created to stay the same form
our entire life."

"I'm not sure I can let go of my old life," I sighed.

"oh you simply must," the cloud whispered in my ear.
"because once you release what you used to be
and embrace who you are meant to be now—
something amazing will happen," the cloud said

"what's that?" I asked while looking at my hands that were beginning to billow
and shapeshift.

"you'll start to float."

and with that my feet lifted off the ground

www.johnroedel.com

. . .

Appendix

Resources

. . .

Appendix

Resources

For help, call 211. This is a national resource line staffed 24/7 with trained counselors. You can dial "211" in any U.S. state and they will direct you to the appropriate resources in your state.

Books

- *The 7 Principles for Making Marriage Work,* by Dr. John Gottman (Research findings on what works and what doesn't for communication and connection)

- *Love Factually: Ten Proven Steps from I Wish to I Do,* by Dr. Duana Welch (The science behind love and dating)

- *The Five Love Languages: The Secret to Love that Lasts,* by Gary Chapman (Speaking the same love language matters.)

- *Attached: The New Science of Adult Attachment and How It Can Help You Find—and Keep—Love,* by Amir Levine and Rachel Heller

- *Too Good to Leave, Too Bad to Stay: A Step-by-Step Guide to Help You Decide Whether to Stay in or Get Out of Your Relationship,* by Mira Kirshenbaum

- *Are You the One for Me?* by Barbara DeAngelis

- *Everything Isn't Terrible: Conquer Your Insecurities, Interrupt Your Anxiety, and Finally Calm Down,* by Dr. Kathleen Smith (The chapter on love is especially insightful.)

- *Uncoupling: Turning Points in Intimate Relationships,* by Diane Vaughan (More of an academic read but fascinating findings on the uncoupling process)

- *Divorced Dads' Rules for Raising* Relatively *Stable Kids,* by Patrick L. Talley

Links

All of these are online at https://tinyurl.com/divorce-links

- Why counseling doesn't work in abusive relationships: https://psychcentral.com/pro/why-couples-counseling-doesnt-work-in-abusive-relationships

- Get help sorting out whether a relationship is abusive—read articles or contact via live chat, text, or phone: https://www.loveisrespect.org

- The secret to love is kindness: https://www.theatlantic.com/health/archive/2014/06/happily-ever-after/372573/

- She Divorced Me Because I Left Dishes by the Sink: https://www.huffpost.com/entry/she-divorced-me-i-left-dishes-by-the-sink_b_9055288

- Relationship red flags and why we ignore them: https://www.livewellwithsharonmartin.com/relationship-red-flags/

- Safety and the brain, by Al Turtle: https://www.alturtle.com/archives/1239

- The research on predicting divorce, by Dr. John Gottman: https://www.gottman.com/blog/the-research-predicting-divorce-from-an-oral-history-interview/

- Esther Perel: https://www.estherperel.com/focus-on-categories/communication-and-connection

- Mark Manson's relationship advice compilation: https://markmanson.net/relationship-advice

- Dr. Nicole LePera on Instagram: @the.holistic.psychologist: https://www.instagram.com/the.holistic.psychologist/

- Reddit's marriage resources: https://www.reddit.com/r/Marriage/wiki/index

- Tiffany Roe's podcast *Therapy Thoughts:* https://tiffanyroe.com/blogs/therapy-thoughts-podcast

- Love is not a mystery: https://onwisconsin.uwalumni.com/features/love-is-not-a-mystery/

- Understanding emotional regulation: https://www.betterhelp.com/advice/general/what-is-emotional-regulation/

- Learn about Nonviolent Communication (NVC), also known as Compassionate Communication: https://positivepsychology.com/non-violent-communication/

- "The Power of Apology" by Robert Gordon: https://www.youtube.com/watch?v=R7vP01U8qr4

Community

- See Reddit's divorce and relationship groups:

  - ☐ https://www.reddit.com/r/Divorce/

  - ☐ https://www.reddit.com/r/relationship_advice/

  - ☐ https://www.reddit.com/r/KindVoice/

  - ☐ (Or search by keyword to find a group of interest)

- Facebook: https://tinyurl.com/divorce-stories

About the Author

Holly Russo is passionate about helping people live more fulfilling lives. She's a trained educator by The Gottman Institute, a renowned research organization that focuses on relationship dynamics and communication. She has spent more than 10 years studying the nuances of connection and partnership. She lives her own happily rebuilt life with her husband in the Maryland suburbs of D.C. This is her debut book, largely fueled by chocolate and hugs from the dog. For more information, visit her website, On Rebuilding at https://onrebuilding.com.

www.ingramcontent.com/pod-product-compliance
Lightning Source LLC
Chambersburg PA
CBHW070808280326
41934CB00012B/3114